HIDDEN TREASURES

DUDLEY

Edited by Steve Twelvetree

First published in Great Britain in 2002 by
YOUNG WRITERS
Remus House,
Coltsfoot Drive,
Peterborough, PE2 9JX
Telephone (01733) 890066

HB ISBN 0 75433 764 2
SB ISBN 0 75433 765 0

FOREWORD

This year, the Young Writers' Hidden Treasures competition proudly presents a showcase of the best poetic talent from over 72,000 up-and-coming writers nationwide.

Young Writers was established in 1991 and we are still successful, even in today's technologically-led world, in promoting and encouraging the reading and writing of poetry.

The thought, effort, imagination and hard work put into each poem impressed us all, and once again, the task of selecting poems was a difficult one, but nevertheless, an enjoyable experience.

We hope you are as pleased as we are with the final selection and that you and your family continue to be entertained with *Hidden Treasures Dudley* for many years to come.

CONTENTS

The Poems

The Horrible Sight

It's not a pleasant sight,
It should have a home,
'It's not completely worthless,'
You hear the people moan.

The young boy at the park,
His mates have had a fight,
They knock the litter bin over
And it shows up in the light.

The mother pushing child along,
'It's everywhere I look
The rubbish, it is building up,
It's even in the brook.'

So all we have to do
Is put it in the bin,
Then the world will be
As clean as a brand new pin.

The father playing Sunday golf
Says, 'It's so very well known,
The bin's the place to put it,
It has a special home.'

The young girl playing at her nan's,
'We all must do our part,
It is making the world look a mess,
So we have to make a start.'

So all we have to do
Is put it in the bin,
Then the world will be
As clean as a brand new pin.

Jonathan Harris (10)
Amblecote Primary School

Pollution Is Back In The Ocean

Pollution in the blue ocean,
Spreading like sun lotion.
Sea creatures are hiding fast,
They'd better move in a flash.

Pollution, it is coming now,
We need to stop it, but how?

The tanker spills its thick, black oil,
The animals are dying.
'Help us now, this is your mess.'
The creatures are all crying.

Pollution, it is coming now,
We need to stop it, but how?

Rachel Treece (10)
Amblecote Primary School

Gemma

I have got a cousin, Gemma
And she is very windy,
She likes Sindy,
She loves Teletubbies.

She is really funny
And dresses like a bunny,
When she goes to sleep
Throws her food around the room
And plays with her toy broom.

Ben Mead (10)
Amblecote Primary School

Deforestation

As the fierce diggers come
And the dazzling fires arrive,
All the animals scatter,
Not much will survive.

As the trees crash
And the axes chop,
The animals scuttle,
Out of the trees they drop.

The house plans are laid,
There're homes for everyone,
But the animals have no place to sleep,
Because the forest's gone.

Sam Lavender (10)
Amblecote Primary School

Smoking

Smoking gives you cancer,
It pollutes the air,
Smoke gets everywhere,
People beware!

Fags aren't great,
When you get ill,
Obviously you might die,
Cigarettes just kill.

Lorna MacGregor (10)
Amblecote Primary School

It's Everywhere

When you go to town,
Do you look around?
Bubblegum on the pavement,
Papers on the floor,
Overflowing dustbins,
Dog-ends more and more.

You can stop this disaster,
Don't let pollution be your master!

When you go to town,
Do you look around?
Car fumes spinning,
Keeps on killing,
Fumes all around,
Death makes no sound.

You can stop this disaster,
Don't let pollution be your master.

Sophie Richards (10)
Amblecote Primary School

Execution

In the middle of the jungle,
Loud noises arrive,
The animals they all run off,
Not many will survive.

The hunters come,
To the darkened trees,
Animals rush round and shout,
'Don't hurt us anymore please.'

The whales keep on vanishing,
Koala, pandas too,
Hunters come with big huge guns,
Soon they'll only be in the zoo.

Ceiran Talbot (10)
Amblecote Primary School

DANGER ANIMALS!

The drastic killing of animals
In the world today,
Pollution, litter,
Danger animals!
Why doesn't the madness pay?
It won't for a year or two
But really, it matters.

Why are we doing this?
We are silly living things,
All I know is that this is madness,
I will stop this in a bit,
Stupid creatures destroy, destroy and destroy.

Rainforests obsolete,
Tribes with no joy,
Animals in despair,
No hope, no life to spare.

Goodbye to the trees,
So green and so fine,
Goodbye home sweet home,
Destroyed in its pride.

Jordan Young (11)
Amblecote Primary School

Something Happened In The Night!

It felt like I was walking on clouds.

When I got out of bed and pulled up my blind,
I saw big balls of cotton wool.

I was so excited, I put my coat on and my boots
And ran outside.

Round the flowerpot, it looked like crystals.

The snowman my friends had made, shone,
It looked like it had glitter on.

My heart was beating fast.

I made a snow angel in the snow
And when I stood up and looked back at it,
It looked like fizzy lemonade.

I made a snowman,
It shone in the sun
Like crystal.

Amy Kelly (8)
Amblecote Primary School

Where Have They All Gone?

The great green rainforest is leaving,
It's never coming back,
The animals are evacuating,
Running from the lumberjack.

The koala is about to go,
The dodo's already gone,
The crocks are swimming crazily,
Looking for something to feed on.

Where have the pandas vanished to?
Why have they all left?
The crock has left the lake,
It's all just one big theft.

Matthew Squire (10)
Amblecote Primary School

HELP!

Poor, needy robin,
Collapses on the ground,
Dying of a painful death,
But still it makes no sound.

Slow, grazing sheep,
Keel over in great pain,
This monster keeps on killing,
A burning, blazing flame.

Even helpless fish,
That do to us no harm,
Are murdered by this poison,
No one's feeling calm.

The world is slowly dying,
But no one can escape,
A horrific sort of killing,
You're so scared you start to shake

And all the helpless creatures,
Let rip of a terrible yelp,
'Please . . .
Help!'

Jodie Evans (10)
Amblecote Primary School

Snow And Snow

In the night the gentle snow fell
Like a polar bear walking
In my garden, in the morning
I went out, I was amazed

When I went outside,
I saw a polar bear's tail
I ran and ran after it
And started to lose my house

I remembered I lost the polar bear
So I found my way back home
I told my mum I saw
A polar bear

'No you didn't' she said
'Yes I did' I replied
'Show me' she said
So I showed her
The glittery white snow.

Jason Crowther (8)
Amblecote Primary School

What's Going On?

Pollution is killing animals,
All over the ocean,
Whenever a tanker crashes,
Oil is spread, like a potion.

Sewage is on the way,
It's coming out to sea.
It's starting to stench dreadfully,
It cannot happen to be!

Sammy Wyatt (10)
Amblecote Primary School

Execution

The poachers are coming,
Blasting their way through,
Raising their guns,
In the morning dew.

The animals hear the news,
The birds scatter away,
There're too many dying,
There's nothing more to say.

The poachers quickly nearing,
The rhinos dying out,
'The pandas disappearing fast!'
You hear the creatures shout.

The animals are dying,
Whilst the poachers come,
The creatures are all dying out,
In the morning sun.

Daniel Liversidge (10)
Amblecote Primary School

THE BLACK GIANT!

Spreading like wildfire,
Quickly dispersing,
A blue wilderness,
But not for long,
Would it stay blue,
    or clear
    or even a pleasant place to be?

From whales to plankton all seemed to me
All very scared of what was to be.

The giant spilled his thick, black blood,
Killing everything,
Nothing should really come too close,
A blanket of thick, black, oozing oil,
Choking everything.

From whales to plankton all seemed to me
All very scared of what was to be.

Thomas Green (10)
Amblecote Primary School

HELP THE WHALES

Faster than lightning,
Quicker than a flash,
Whales are perishing
From floating trash.

So please cooperate
And save the species,
Don't leave it too late
To pick up the pieces.

Daniel Tandy (10)
Amblecote Primary School

LITTER

Litter, litter everywhere
Where I walk
And where I stare
All in the streets
And everywhere
It's very untidy and cruel

Litter, litter everywhere
It belongs in bins
So do bottle tops
And tins
So do not drop it, please I say

Litter, litter everywhere
If only you could see a nice
And tidy environment
It would be so much better
For you and me.

Jodie Goodall (11)
Amblecote Primary School

The Swan

While I was away, it started to snow,
It snowed big, heavy cotton wool balls,
Thundering down on the ground,
I felt amazed and shocked.

It covered the ground like a big, white swan,
Its down feathers were all gently cleaned and washed.

It looked beautiful,
The swan's eyes shone like crystals
And gleamed like big diamonds.

Chloe Jagpal (9)
Amblecote Primary School

My Brother, Matthew

He likes Pokémon and Digimon too,
He likes pizza when he's hungry,
He is bossy and rough at home
And sometimes we fight.

He is quiet in the playground and in class,
He is usually happy, but sometimes he's sad,
He plays on his computer and Nintendo 64
And he's funny when he watches the Disney Channel
Sitting on the floor!

Luke Heath (10)
Amblecote Primary School

My Cousin, Emily

I have a cousin, Emily,
She's nine months old,
She is as funny as a bunny,
Except when she has a cold,
She likes biting then hiding from me.

She likes rolling across the floor,
She kicks and licks,
She likes wriggling and then tickling,
She eats her pudding and then starts to cry.

She likes sleeping and she likes weeping,
She likes playing,
She likes sneezing,
She is a funny little thing.

Laura Fellows (10)
Amblecote Primary School

The Parrot's Point Of View

Tractors,
Strange people,
Animals dying needlessly,
Homes disappearing,
Extinction closing in,
My forest?
Your furniture?
You choose!

Charlotte Millward (10)
Amblecote Primary School

WHITEWASH

Snow falls down, down,
Down,
On the gentle ground.
It
Nestles on the blade of
Grass.
Sometimes it is pretty.
Sometimes it is slushy
And horrible.
But sometimes it is the most
Beautiful
Thing you have seen.
Snow
Is like gems and diamonds
Twinkling
On the ground.
Snow
Is like a polar bear
Lying on
The grass.
Snow is like ermine.
Snow
Is a piece of
Paper
Rolled out.
Snow is fun.

Kiran Jagpal (9)
Amblecote Primary School

Hidden Treasure

Through the icy seas,
Deep under the ocean,
Is where I live.

A wreck of the Armada, laying on the ocean sands,
It was dark, creepy, spooky like a shadow hunting me,
I glided in slowly like a feather in the air,
But what I found was extraordinary.

An octopus awake, really scary now,
I grabbed a handful of what was inside the chest,
I swam off as fast as I could,
Do you want to know what was inside?
Gold, glistening treasure,
Millions have died from dangerous fish
Or they just drown,
I could have died but I survived.

Stacey Hickman (10)
Bromley Pensnett Primary School

Hidden Treasure

I went under the water,
Down,
Down,
Down.
In front of me I saw a starfish,
Octopus and a dolphin, rubble
And I saw bubbles from a wreck.
Enter the wreck, find the treasure,
Look at it, it's evil, leave it alone,
Leave it alone.

Paul Jenkins (9)
Bromley Pensnett Primary School

HIDDEN TREASURE

I went under the sea,
To find hidden treasure,
I had seen all the animals under the sea,
I went to find the treasure,
A big, ugly octopus guarding it,
I went round the back,
The treasure was sticking out,
I grabbed the treasure
And swam back up to the air.

I climbed up to the sand,
Where the air is fresh,
I had found the hidden treasure,
I placed it on the sand,
Where the crowd was screaming,
But beneath the sea,
Crying,
Crying,
Crying,
Just for me,
The treasure lost to me.

Kirsty Jones (9)
Bromley Pensnett Primary School

HIDDEN TREASURE

As I set off I heard church bells,
Halfway, the clatter of shells,
Heard echoes in the distance,
My heart raced, I waited until a wave came,
When it arrived, I jumped in,
I just heard the bubbles dancing.

I saw a wrecked ship, I was horrified,
Then I looked inside,
There was a treasure box,
When I looked there was sparkling gold,
I got back to the ship,
Every second seemed like a dream.

Bonnie Oakley (10)
Bromley Pensnett Primary School

HIDDEN TREASURE

I place myself into the submarine,
Suddenly people start to push through the sand and into the sea,
As I drift away slowly,
Waves splash upon me,
I can see bubbles rising,
So I go under the sea,
But what do I see?
Sharks feasting upon some fish,
Stingrays disguising themselves,
Electric eels flashing bright,
Then something catches my eye,
I look and I see a chest covered by an octopus,
I try to move it but it won't budge,
So I put on my diving suit,
But then I looked at the air pocket, there was only very little,
I had a choice to go out or to stay in the submarine,
I stood for a moment,
The right choice was to stay in,
Not to spread the secrets of the deep,
Never to be discovered.

Louis Tibbetts (9)
Bromley Pensnett Primary School

HIDDEN TREASURE!

Under the sea,
To look at all the animals, dolphins and sharks,
See some treasure,
Hidden in a big box,
Gold and silver.

There were octopus and sharks, ugly and fat,
With one eye,
So big I couldn't see a thing,
Sharks chased me and I swam up to the surface with the treasure,
I opened the treasure and looked in,
I gazed out at the treasure,
Amazing!
The animals swam up
And tried to get the treasure,
I pulled and pulled,
I grabbed tight and pulled,
It fell
Into the water,
I screamed.

Terri Johnson (10)
Bromley Pensnett Primary School

HIDDEN TREASURE

The dark, dark sea,
It shone like crystals,
I saw a shark, it chased a fish,
It was gone in a flash,
The box was shining,
It was made of gold,

Filled with jewellery,
Flashes in the light,
I glided slowly through the sea,
I saw a whale, it saw me,
It came to me and sidled me back,
I lost some of the treasure.

Lisa Bradley (9)
Bromley Pensnett Primary School

HIDDEN TREASURE

Under water, ocean water,
1901 and I was very scared,
There were sharks everywhere,
Big ones, little ones, but I didn't care,
There was a beautiful dolphin, grey as armour
On a soldier, strong as can be,
The dolphin swerved around me,
Suddenly I saw an octopus, fat, spotty, scary,
It looked at me and stood like a fairy,
Then suddenly in front of my eyes there was
Hidden treasure, gold, diamonds and jewellery,
Sharks, octopuses guarding it,
Must have been a tidal wave and it moved
And nobody knew, I thought as it lit,
I was shocked and flabbergasted,
I looked at it and didn't think it had lasted,
I picked it up, a shark nipped me,
'Oh no!' I said 'it needs a key.'
I brought it to shore and I was a hero.

Kirstie Bavington (9)
Bromley Pensnett Primary School

HIDDEN TREASURE

Swimming with dolphins,
Swimming with dolphins,
It's a treasure to me,
Their skin so shiny,
Their skin so smooth.

Their skin so grey as a pencil lead,
They flop their tails proudly,
We swim to the surface,
They squeak sweetly,
Every second I feel as if it's a dream,
It's a massive treasure to me,
I wish I were a dolphin and could swim with them every day,
It's the only treasure I would have,
I'd rather swim with dolphins than have a thousand pounds,
Now you know I love dolphins, it's a big value to me,
But the pleasure is being with dolphins.

Jade Field (9)
Bromley Pensnett Primary School

HIDDEN TREASURE

Under the blue sea,
There will be,
A treasure box,
I saw a fish with spotty socks,
Then I saw a king,
With a golden ring
On his finger,
Then I heard a singer,

Then the singer gave me a key,
We were proud, my friend and me,
Then we swam to the treasure box,
We saw a shark with chicken pox,
We finally got there to the treasure box,
We opened it and it had a thousands pounds in it
And a lot of jewellery,
We were rich for ever and ever.

Lucy Hickman (9)
Bromley Pensnett Primary School

The Magical Box

I found in the box:

A crystal dolphin jumping in and out of the waves,
A flock of golden fish going around and around in circles,
A diamond shell lying on the sand in the hot sun.

I found in the box:

A sharp toenail from a golden dragon breathing fire,
A shiny tooth from a scary dinosaur in the woods,
A white and sharp horn from a really fast unicorn.

I found in the box:

The planet Saturn, with its rings going round and round,
A really bright star shining like the sun,
A dark green alien, walking like a duck.

This box is made from gold and silver,
A golden star stuck on the box,
Some shiny seashells stuck all around.

Alex Higgs (9)
Colley Lane Primary School

Sunken Treasure

When it was dropped into the sea,
Something was in it, what could it be?
Was it a ghost? Was it some tea
Or was it treasure for you and me?

Maybe if we had looked around,
We might have found a key on the ground.
We couldn't open it and we all frowned,
So we put it back without a sound.

Sam Fowkes (9)
Colley Lane Primary School

Under The Sea

Under the deep, deep sea,
Came a fish with a crown,
The fish with a crown,
Had a very nasty frown,
So his parents told me!

Abigail Ward (7)
Colley Lane Primary School

Sea

S ea is a place where fishes swim
E els slithering about ready to electrocute
A ngelfish floating angelically in the water.

Josephine Mills (8)
Colley Lane Primary School

THE DREAMS OF A CLEANER BOY!

Swishing and swaying through the sea,
Now nobody can catch me,
A stumble of feet as I land on the sand
And with a fish I come hand in hand,
Bubbles of water now crowd me
And out the corner of my eye I see . . .
Diamonds and rubies that twirl,
A great white, beautiful pearl,
Gold fit for a king,
A shellfish that can sing,
Birthstones scattered across the chest,
But am I really set free, can I rest?
Slowly I open my eyes,
Captain pulls me out of bed as a surprise,
Scrub those decks, life's not easy peasy,
I suppose he's right, dreams don't come easy!

April Phillips (11)
Colley Lane Primary School

SMOKEY, MY RABBIT

Smokey is my pet
Sometimes he gets upset
Smokey has a new hutch
He likes it very much
Sometimes he makes me frown
When he turns his bowl upside down
Sometimes he won't do as he's told
Sometimes he's as good as gold.
He's my treasure.

Ashley Parrish (8)
Colley Lane Primary School

THE HIDDEN TREASURE CHEST

We found a treasure map in the sea,
I thought, oh that's good fun for me.

We set out a trail for us to follow,
For the treasure for us to find in which we will wallow.

Rich we will be,
For everyone to see.

We will dig high and low
And swimming we will go.

Searching the sea bed,
For where the treasure map led.

Jewels and coins, gold and pearls, diamonds and crowns
Were the treasure we found at the bottom of the sea.

Kirstie Till (10)
Colley Lane Primary School

HIDDEN TREASURE

There are no clues,
There are no signs,
Just an old map of dungeons and mines.
So off we go with a torch and a stick,
Smashing down brambles,
Come thin or come thick.
At last we reach where X marks the spot -
We've finally reached the golden pot.
We've found the hidden treasure that will make us rich,
But first we must get it out of this great big ditch.

Shane Shaw (8)
Colley Lane Primary School

Hidden Treasures

Deep, deep under the sea,
Where hidden treasures hide,
There hidden in a secret box,
For no one ever to find.

They twinkle and sparkle
And they always shine,
They're gold and silver,
I wish they were mine.

They wait and wait,
For a pirate to come,
To grab them all,
So they can be done.

One day a pirate
Will find the treasure
And he will shout with joy,
'They will be mine forever!'

Masera Baazab (11)
Colley Lane Primary School

My Treasure

My treasure is my mum
She's there when I fall
She's there when I call
She's there to feed me
And when I need her
I love my treasure
My mum.

Amy Skitt (9)
Colley Lane Primary School

THE TREASURE CHEST

I opened the box
I opened my eyes
When I looked inside
What a big surprise

Lots of jewels
Lots of gold
I cupped my hands
To take a hold

The jewels shone bright
The gold was the best
I lay down beside it
To take a rest

This was my dream
This is the best
At last I've found
A treasure chest!

Amy Thomas (8)
Colley Lane Primary School

HIDDEN TREASURES

Under the sea there is treasure,
Buried under the sand,
Down under the deep ground where people can measure stuff,
People are buried under there,
People can look for treasure.

Laura Ellis (8)
Colley Lane Primary School

LAKE TREASURE

In dark woodland,
Trees gently sway,
I'm far from home,
I'm miles away.
The fragrant grass,
Is dew shrouded
And the sparkling lake,
Is rose surrounded.

I dive into
The gleaming deep
And marvelling
At what I see,
A rainbow shoal,
At which I stare
And is it . . . treasure
I see there?

I grab it
And take a look,
Is it me or has it shook?
My mind feels
Trapped in a maze,
Then all disappears,
In a rainbow haze . . .

I've just woke in my bed
And from my pocket pull,
A diamond, glittering! But . . . how?

Christine Stafford (10)
Colley Lane Primary School

HIDDEN TREASURES

In the furthest corner,
Past the flower beds,
Surrounded by orangey
Brown walls,
Hidden is:

Red, silky flowers petals,
Surrounded by twinkling grass,
Dazzling sun.

Robins singing,
Trees swaying
To the song of the wind,
Flowers dance like ballerinas,
Everywhere you walk.

Garden gnomes chatter
Around the clear blue pond,
Swing on the old crooked swing.

Jamie Lad (11)
Dingle Primary School

HIDDEN TREASURE

In a secret place,
Where no one else has been,
Lies a crumbling treasure chest,
That only I have seen.

It has gold, silver,
Rubies and gems,
Crocodiles swim,
Round and round.

I count and count,
But still I doubt,
What will happen,
When I'm out.

Jennifer Marsh (10)
Dingle Primary School

HIDDEN TREASURES

Rubies red,
Sparkling diamonds,
Beautiful jewels,
They're all hidden in my secret place,
My big, emerald, bushy tree,
Full of hidden treasures,
No one knows they're there,
Except for me,
Glamorous hair beads,
Glitzy statues,
Pretty petals,
Gorgeous as can be,
No one knows they're there,
Except for me,
Pink pearls,
Gold books,
Finished with a line of jade,
Silver flowers,
Lime leaves,
It's ever so pretty in there,
Maybe in the future I might tell someone,
Tell someone about my secret place,
If I don't I will still be happy with my
Hidden treasure.

Samantha Bagley (10)
Dingle Primary School

Hidden Treasures

I have got a secret place,
In a cave on the beach,
I go there every day,
To make sure nobody else goes in.

In the secret place,
There is a treasure chest,
It's full of gold, silver, rubies and diamonds,
But the chest itself is old, gold and very dusty,
But I don't mind.

I check it every day,
To see if everything's there,
Wait a minute, where's the key?
It's nowhere to be seen.

Crunch! What was that?
Oh no, it's a pirate
And he's getting away
I've got to stop him.

He gets in his ship and sails away,
I can't catch him anymore.
I go to my cave
And push the big, grey, rough rock
As hard as I can,
It's locked forever.

Roxanne Ward (10)
Dingle Primary School

Treasure

All alone on an island
With loads of buried treasure
And under the sea
And at the other side is an old house

Lots of beasts and dinosaurs
In the chest is rubies and gold
Yes I'm rich
But I wish I was at home.

Adam Fellows (10)
Dingle Primary School

UNDER THE SEA IN THE SAND

Splish, splash goes the sea,
The dancing mermaids brushing their hair,
I look under the sea,
I see something glistening,
I dive down but the sparkling has gone,
Fish tickle my feet,
I try to move the sharks that are guarding the treasure,
The sharks finally move, but there is a stingray lying on it,
It moves,
I dig up the sand,
The seahorses are bobbing up and down,
I lift up the lid off the rusty box,
I'm really shocked - hidden treasure!
Glistening crowns, beautiful pearls,
Red rubies, oh and what's this?
An old crumbling brown envelope,
What is it?
It's a map,
But what is it for?
Where does it lead to?
Splish, splash goes the sea.

Jenny Johnson (11)
Dingle Primary School

[F]INDING TREASURE

T o find treasure
R ead a treasure map,
E nemy is near,
A ll sights clear,
S hould be the right place,
U nder the sand,
R eal money everywhere,
E veryone's rich.

Rhys Gater (10)
Dingle Primary School

HIDDEN TREASURES

T reassure is hidden.
R eading the map.
E verywhere I look to find my treasure
A nd I don't find it.
S hh! I can hear someone coming!
U nder the ground it's hidden.
R unning to get it.
E nd of adventure.
S tart another treasure hunt!

Adam Staves (9)
Dingle Primary School

HIDDEN TREASURE

A big colourful box under my soft, comfy bed,
Jewellery that sparkled is now bound to be dusty.
Locked away secretly with a special golden lock,
With so many memories,
I can't remember them,

A wooden old box,
As rusty as an old car,
Beautiful jewellery, silver or gold,
Photos of friends and family that's never been looked at before,
Old memories, so old.

Heather Walker (11)
Dingle Primary School

HIDDEN TREASURE

T o find hidden treasure
R ead a map,
E verybody's after it.
A ll clear, nothing here,
S houldn't it be here
U nder the sand?
R ubies everywhere,
E verbody's rich!

William Yarnall (10)
Dingle Primary School

HIDDEN TREASURE

You can look in California or right on the spot
You can look in a place or down the drain
You can look in alleys or down in the valleys
You can look in the sea or up in a tree
You can look on a train or in the rain
You can look underground, they'll never be found
For my treasure is my nan and grandad.

Sean Ward (8)
Dingle Primary School

You Found Something

You found a necklace,
You found a pearl,
You found a golden bowl,
You found a necklace,
You found a pearl,
You found a golden girl.
You found a necklace,
You found a pearl,
You found a golden chair.
You found a necklace,
You found a pearl,
You found a golden glass pearl.

You found this and that.
Now you have found
Your hidden treasures.

Rebecca Ettle (10)
Dingle Primary School

Hidden Treasure

Ten pirates sail across the sea
And look at their map on their knee,
They laugh and shout and drink lots of beer,
The pirates all say they are getting near.
To dig for their lovely treasure,
Then they can live in lots of pleasure.
They have silver, rubies and some gold
And then their ship can be sold.

Rhianna Davies (9)
Dingle Primary School

HIDDEN TREASURES

Somewhere out there
Is an island
And my mission is
To find it somehow,
I will not fail.
As I got into the sea,
I started to swim,
When the sea got deeper,
I felt the really strong tide
Taking me in a direction.
It got even deeper, I had to rest,
As soon as I stopped I heard
Whistling whales sounding like they
Were telling me something,
Like which way to go.
Dolphins swam around me,
I looked in deeply,
All I could see was black.
The sea is an explosion of blue ink.
When I went underwater,
I saw magic rocks, shiny shells,
Above me I saw the waves crashing up the rocks.
There it was,
The hidden island,
It was silent and graceful,
I swam to shore,
I touched the sand,
There I stayed,
With the palm trees
And the fish.

Kirstie Baker (11)
Dingle Primary School

The Front Door

Early one white winter's morn
Came Connie and her unicorn
She knocked upon the great front door
Of greedy giant Gobblemour
The giant, stirring in his bed
Rubbed his eyes, scratched his head
Who dares to wake Gobblemour?
He roars whilst opening the door
Then he saw Connie plus her unicorn
Now though he'd gorged the night before
He hungered still
Greedy Gobblemour.

Jasmine Morris (10)
Dingle Primary School

Hidden Treasures

Sparkling sea
Deep water
Golden silky sand
Dolphins dance round
The old dark chest
Wrapped in slimy seaweed
Opens with a creak
Silver and gold rings

I swim back up to the magic land
I swim past the rough rocks
And the shiny shells.

Elizabeth Sant (10)
Dingle Primary School

TREASURE OF THE SEA

There is a treasure at the bottom of the sea
Which looks most beautifully
There is a treasure at the bottom of the sea
Which shines like gold
There is a treasure at the bottom of the sea
Which is worth a million pounds to me
There is a treasure at the bottom of the sea
Which I love most dearly
There is a treasure at the bottom of the sea
Please bring it back to me
There is a treasure at the bottom of the sea
It's no ordinary treasure, oh no, it's the heart of the sea!

Bethany Strong (9)
Dingle Primary School

HIDDEN TREASURE

In the dark blue sea
Tatty sunken ships
Sharks protect
In the freezing cold water
Terrible feelings come to his mind
Dreaming of treasure
Tongue dangling
Minute silence
Smells treasure
Almost faints
But stays strong because
Of the precious gold.

Matthew Baxter (10)
Dingle Primary School

UNDER MY BED

Under my bed was dark and gloomy,
Cobwebs about,
Spiders were crawling,
Wooden boards across the top of the dark old rusty hinges,
Finding black and white pictures,
Peeling them from under the planks holding the bed up,
Bright light on my watch helping me see my old belongings,
I placed the pictures face-way up,
I peered my eyes at the doddery black and white mouldy pictures,
A young man,
Didn't know who it was,
I looked closely,
One bit of writing in the corner . . .
April 12th 1789,
My grandad.
It looked vulnerable,
Under my bed it was dark and gloomy,
Cobwebs were about,
Spiders were crawling,
Light was fading away off my watch,
Dreaming . . . what will my life end as?

Edward Derek Sidaway (11)
Dingle Primary School

HIDDEN TREASURES

Pirates, pirates all over the world
Burying treasure anywhere they please
They bury treasure on islands in sea
They bury it everywhere that eyes can see
They bury it in trees, in leaves, then they go back for more.

Adam Chance (9)
Dingle Primary School

My Secret

A box
Full of hidden treasure
Old and dusty treasures
All at the back of a house
Broken windows
Slippery floorboards
A box
I look inside and see
Secret stones
Enchanted photos
Books and diaries
Crimpled letters
I find dusty medals
I feel a mysterious wind
In the box
There're old memories.

Samantha Kings (10)
Dingle Primary School

A Counting Poem

One orange octopus
Two tiny turtles
Three tiny tiger fish
Four fat fish
Five tiny fish
Six shiny starfish
Seven smelly sea snails
Eight empty eels
Nine naughty nuns
Ten tiny tadpoles.

Jade Francis (7)
Dingle Primary School

HIDDEN TREASURE

Dolphins dive
Rocks are rough
Washing waves
Silky sand
Sparkling treasure
Bold brown box
Treasure island
Prickly palm trees
Red pearls
Golden leaf
Famous letter
Dolphins dive
Rocks are rough
Washing waves
Silky sand.

Rachelle Sawyer (10)
Dingle Primary School

HIDDEN TREASURE

This treasure is a secret,
It might be hidden in the sea,
It might be hidden in a tree,
It could be hidden in a hole,
It could be hidden with a mole,
It would be hidden in a crib,
It would be hidden with a bib,
You won't find it there,
You won't find it here
Because it is my baby sister.

Jordan Danks (8)
Dingle Primary School

Hidden Treasure

Under the sea in
A far, far away place
Mermaids are swaying
Crying dolphins
Glimmering whales
Some treasure lies on a
Velvet cushion
Bronze, gold and silver
Down, down dark and darker
Into the smelly boat
Some white jaws shine
In front of me
I'm gone forever and ever.

Melissa Tonks (10)
Dingle Primary School

Hidden Treasure

My treasure is far and wide
My treasure you will never find
You can look inside the leaves
Or up in the trees
It's too precious to let go
Do you want to know a secret?
I'll give you a clue
It lives in my house
And it squawks
No, it's not a bird
But it's my baby sister, Meredith.

Hannah Penn (8)
Dingle Primary School

HIDDEN TREASURE

I find the treasure,
Take it home,
Put it in my secret dome.
I know a secret that nobody else knows
And I'm going to put it where no one ever goes.
I find the secret place, somehow
And I hide it here,
Here and now.
I go home and watch TV,
I even visit my granny,
But even if I do the best things,
I won't forget about the joy
The treasure brings.

Jessica Thompson-Webb (9)
Dingle Primary School

I KNOW A SECRET

I know a secret nobody knows.
I know a secret I'm not to tell.
I know a secret my own place.
I know a secret, where it is.
I know a secret, I'll give you a clue.
I know a secret you don't know.
I know a secret you'll never know.
I know a secret I'll never tell.
I know a secret, it's my treasure!

Gabriella Ragno (10)
Dingle Primary School

Hidden Treasure

Lying in the sand
It's staying there
Where nobody can find it
And no one is there
Dark in the ocean
Where whales swim
With a big dark fin covering it there
So nobody can find it
And no one is there
With one foot in the ocean
And one foot in the air
That's where my treasure is standing.

Rebekah Garbett (9)
Dingle Primary School

Look

Look down the well,
Look down the back of the settee,
Look down the road,
Look down the garden,
Look down the river,
Look down the hole,
Look down the stairs,
Look down the pit,
Look down the loo,
Look down the street,
Can you find the treasure?

Ryan Smith (10)
Dingle Primary School

FINDING TREASURE

There was a young lad named Jack
And he was very sad.
He had a pup named Zup and he was very bad.
One day he was sailing,
But his ship was holey.
So he ended up bailing out,
He got washed up with his pup
And said 'Hey up, what's that?'
It was a map for hidden treasure.
He started to dig a very big hole
And then he met a mole and said,
'Do you know where to go
To find the hidden treasure?'
'That way,' he said
And then he said 'I'm going to bed.'
Then they found a chest
And in it was a vest.

Michael Mobberley (9)
Dingle Primary School

HIDDEN TREASURE

You can look under sea,
I will give you a clue, but you'll never know,
It's someone in London,
I will tell you because you still don't know,
It's someone very special to me,
Just keep it a secret and I'll tell you,
It's my uncle, he's special.

Daniel Rock (9)
Dingle Primary School

HIDDEN TREASURE

H iding in the sea
I t's lying there
D rowning in the sand
D umb as anything, just lying there
E veryone trying to find it
N ever to be found

T reasure, treasure, treasure
R eady and waiting
E veryone found it
A t last, got it
S ure we'll sell it they said
U nder the big black flag
R eady to be sold
E nd.

Adam Wheeler (9)
Dingle Primary School

HIDDEN TREASURE

There is treasure you can find
It will stay in your mind
Unless you look, get off the hook
Just pick up your map
Look high and low
Look from arm to toe
Look in the air
All over there
You won't find it there
North or west you look
You will find my treasure in a book.

Daniel Rose (9)
Dingle Primary School

HIDDEN TREASURES

T he treasure's hidden.
R easonably well.
E veryone is searching everywhere.
A s they walk everywhere to find it.
S earching and searching.
U nsure to be found.
R unning everywhere to find it.
E ven if I die.
S earching everywhere, something happens,
They find the treasure!

Jenna Smith (9)
Dingle Primary School

HIDDEN TREASURE

You can't find it in the sea
You can't find it in a tree
You can't find it in the sand
You can't find it under the ground
Because it is locked in my heart.

Jessica Hinman (8)
Dingle Primary School

HIDDEN TREASURE

There is a treasure that you will find
There is a treasure that will glisten in your mind
There is a treasure of gold in a mine
There is a treasure of silver and it's mine.

Joe Crook (8)
Dingle Primary School

HIDDEN TREASURE

I know what you know but do you know what I know?
It's something in my heart,
They cheer me up when I'm low,
They're always being smart,
I know what you know but do you know what I know?
They chase their tails and flop their ears,
One runs round in a wheel,
They don't have any fears,
They're always eating meals,
I know what you know but do you know what I know?
What I know, do you want to know?
Yes.
It's my pets!

Claire Farmer (9)
Dingle Primary School

HIDDEN TREASURE

I know something you don't know,
It's all about my treasure so,
It might be here,
It might be there,
It could be somewhere in the air,
I don't know where,
But I'm most sure it's there,
I'm getting hot, I feel like toast,
The treasure's got to be somewhere,
It's something with four legs,
A wrinkled-up face,
Can you guess?

Bradley Ghent (9)
Dingle Primary School

HIDDEN TREASURE

I know where the treasure is
And you will never know

I know where the treasure is
And you will never know

It might be in the ocean
Or on the sand but

You won't find it near the ground
And I will tell you why

You can't find it, ever
Because it is locked in my body

Forever and ever.

Amelia Hinman (8)
Dingle Primary School

HIDDEN TREASURE

Treasure, treasure, it is all around you,
Careful, careful, it might be under you,
I bet it'll make you sue,
It's rubies, diamonds, brooches, necklaces and gold to,
It's really hard to find because it's very low,
You'll even think about trying roe,
It might be in the tree top,
It will make you call a cop,
I bet you'll think of richy zests
And all that's there is an empty treasure chest.

Elliot Westwood (8)
Dingle Primary School

Hidden Treasure

My treasure, my treasure
Will never be found.
My treasure, my treasure's
Not deep underground.
My treasure, my treasure
Is not high or low.
My treasure will not be where
The river will flow.
My treasure will never go away.

My treasure is not where
The whales dance.
It's not where the trees are,
There isn't a chance.
It's in my home, most unsuspected,
Can you guess it?

Andrew Rogerson (8)
Dingle Primary School

Hidden Treasure

I know a treasure you will not find
I know a treasure you will not find
You can look in a tree or even behind
But you will never find my treasure
You can look west or east or south or north
But you will never find my treasure
Gold, silver, you are wrong, it is not just
Gold and silver, it is the heart of . . .
See, do you want to carry on? OK
My treasure is my stepmum.

Jessica Bird (9)
Dingle Primary School

HIDDEN TREASURE

You can look under rocks
Or up in treetops
Under a tower
Or dig up a flower

Up in the sky
Where aeroplanes fly
But you'll never guess
I must confess

You'll never find
Well I'd die if you had
My mum and dad.

Sarah Potter (8)
Dingle Primary School

A COUNTING POEM

One old orange octopus
Two tired ticklish tadpoles
Three tired tiger sharks
Four thirsty fish
Five fishy Friday fish
Six scary sharks
Seven scary shrimps
Eight electric eels
Nine nasty naughty fish
Ten tiny turtles
Eleven excited eels
Twelve tiny tentacles.

Alison Starkey (8)
Dingle Primary School

HIDDEN TREASURE

H ide that treasure
I n the sand.
D eep down,
D eep down.
E very piece from the
N asty baddies.

T reasure is hidden.
R ich treasure,
E very piece.
A re you pleased?
S uper treasure!
U se that shovel.
R eally exciting,
E xciting!

Thomas Hickman (9)
Dingle Primary School

A COUNTING POEM

One orange octopus,
Two talking troublesome trout,
Three thoughtful tiger sharks,
Four fighting fish,
Five fearsome fossils,
Six sparkling starfish,
Seven sexy shrimps,
Eight electric eels,
Nine naughty newts,
Ten thirsty tortoises.

Laura Taylor (7)
Dingle Primary School

Hidden Treasure

H idden treasure is so great
I t shines like a golden plate,
D oes it have pearls or
D oes it have earls?
E arls and pearls are wonderful things,
N othing can compare to this marvellous thing,

T he treasure is hidden, where could it be?
R eally we want it, don't you as well as we?
E veryone's looking, our gang
A gainst theirs,
S ome people here, some people there,
U nder there, over there,
R ound and round we go,
E verywhere we look, argghh! I found it!

Rosie Bick (10)
Dingle Primary School

A Counting Poem

One octopus
Two turtles
Three jellyfish
Four fish
Five floats
Six seals
Seven starfish
Eight eels
Nine newts
Ten tails.

Kirsty Marsh (7)
Dingle Primary School

HIDDEN TREASURES

H idden treasure,
I think I know where it is.
D ungeon is where the treasure is.
D oom will be waiting.
E lephants will squash you.
N ever let anyone get it.

T ake it to a safe place,
R emember you could be rich!
E lephants might still crush you.
A round the brown set of trees.
S eas will wash the sand off the treasure box.
U se a spade to dig it up.
R ide on a ship to get there.
E lephants still might hurt you.
S ee, you are nearly there!

Rachael Platt (9)
Dingle Primary School

A COUNTING POEM

One old orange octopus
Two ticklish talking trout
Three thirsty thumping turtles
Four falling funny frogs
Five fishy funky fish
Six stinky smelly starfish
Seven silly slinky sharks
Eight electric eels
Nine naughty newts
Ten thousand tadpoles.

Cole Hickman (7)
Dingle Primary School

Hidden Treasures

H idden deep in the ground
I n a very large box was treasure
D ig it up!
D ig it up!
E nemies are waiting
N ever ever will they find it

T ricking smiles on their faces
R eaching for the treasure
E choes everywhere
A ttacking me with golden spears
S ilver guns shooting from the ship
U nder the rubble lie my friends, dead
R ed dripping blood from my legs
E nemies have won
S miling with victory.

Thomas Southall (9)
Dingle Primary School

A Counting Poem

One old starfish
Two big fish
Three fat electric eels
Four black octopus
Five little sharks
Six green bundles of seaweed
Seven great catfish
Eight red fish
Nine naughty electric eels
Ten pink crabs.

Charlotte Yarnall (7)
Dingle Primary School

HIDDEN TREASURE

Treasure, treasure hidden somewhere,
On the bare island I stare.
The awful smell of that well,
Is reeking me out.
Where I stand is just sand,
So if I dig it will be land.
So if I find it, I will hide it
In the place my mum can't find it.
It is in the place no one knows,
Let's have a look in the treasure box.
But all that was in was a fox,
So that was a waste,
For that silly old box.

Sam Harbidge (9)
Dingle Primary School

A COUNTING POEM

One old orange octopus
Two traffic turtles
Three thoughtful treasure maps
Four fighting fish
Five fiddling full fishermen
Six struggling starfish
Seven swimming sleepy Simpsons
Eight empty eels
Nine naughty nails
Ten ticklish tortoises.

Bethany Crump (7)
Dingle Primary School

Hidden Treasure

H idden treasure is a marvellous thing,
I t shines like the top of the Millennium Dome,
D azzling in the wonderful moonlight,
D anger surrounds this wonderful thing,
E verybody wants this magical thing,
N othing can compare to gold

T inkling in the daylight,
R unning people are looking everywhere, over here, over there,
E arls and pearls, rings and earrings
A re all the rage.
S urely you've got some?
U nder the dirt in a chest is the treasure.
R ich people have these things,
E ven you could find it!

Sam Wilkinson (10)
Dingle Primary School

A Counting Poem

One alive octopus
Two talented tadpoles
Three thirsty toads
Four flipping frogs
Five fiddling fish
Six shiny schools
Seven slippery snakes
Eight electric eels
Nine naughty necklaces
Ten ticklish treasures.

Chelsea Love (7)
Dingle Primary School

Hidden Treasure

H ide your treasure,
I n the ground,
D ig it up,
D ead or alive.
E veryone wants it,
N ever give up.

T reasure, treasure, treasure!
R eally good stuff,
E ven if you're sick
A nd very tired.
S earch for treasure in sand or mud,
U nder the sand the treasure will be,
R ubies are the same,
E veryone knows that rubies are as good,
S o now you know what happened.

Danny Broome (9)
Dingle Primary School

A Counting Poem

One orange octopus
Two twirling turtles
Three trendy tiger sharks
Four flying fish
Five fish feet
Six soapy swordfish
Seven sloppy seals
Eight electric eels
Nine knotty newts
Ten thunderous trout.

Stefanie Ward (7)
Dingle Primary School

A Counting Poem

One orange octopus
Two tiny tiger sharks
Three thirsty toads
Four fearful fish
Five famous fish
Six small squids
Seven smelly starfish
Eight enormous eggs
Nine noisy newts
Ten ticklish turtles.

Thomas Garrett (8)
Dingle Primary School

A Counting Poem

One obese octopus
Two tired turtles
Three thirsty toads
Four fearful fish
Five famous frogs
Six singing starfish
Seven small squids
Eight emerging eggs
Nine naughty newts
Ten ticklish tadpoles.

Sophie Dimopoulou (8)
Dingle Primary School

A Counting Poem

One old orange octopus
Two tired ticklish turtles
Three thirsty fish
Four frightening fish
Five fat fish
Six sexy shells
Seven scary skeletons
Eight electric eels
Nine naughty newts
Ten tickly trout.

Thomas Bowen (8)
Dingle Primary School

A Counting Poem

One old orange octopus
Two tired ticklish turtles
Three thirsty tiger sharks
Four frightened fish
Five friendly fish
Six scary sharks
Seven silly swordfish
Eight electric eels
Nine nibbly eels
Ten tiny tentacles.

Rachel Wood (7)
Dingle Primary School

A Counting Poem

One old awkward octopus
Two terrifying tapping turtles
Three thirsty tiny tadpoles
Four floating fighting fish
Five frightened flopping flexible frogs
Six slivering slidey sea snakes
Seven sliding sea starfish
Eight electric excited eels
Nine nipping nasty sharks
Ten tapping talking toads.

Christopher Round (8)
Dingle Primary School

A Counting Poem

One old orange octopus
Two ticklish tickling turtles
Three tidy timpy toads
Four fairy fish
Five furry fish
Six smelly shrimps
Seven silly shells
Eight eating eggs
Nine nibbling newts
Ten ticklish tiger fish.

Chloe Gillard (8)
Dingle Primary School

TREASURE TEDDY

My teddy's the best
He stands out from the rest
He's not scruffy
But he's quite fluffy
I love to clasp him at
My chest because
He's better than the rest!

Grace Audsley (8)
Gig Mill Primary School

THE PAST MEMORY

As the dark purple screams
Ran through me,
Pain struck like lightning,
Hitting a single house,
I couldn't move,
I couldn't move.

Shaking like a boat on
The sea waves,
The dark red blood
Poured from my head,
I thought I had cracked it open,
It smelt like rotten bread,
I couldn't feel my arms or toes,
I couldn't feel them,
I couldn't feel them.

Sarah Holl (10)
Highfields Primary School

The Flowers

The flower's hair was blowing,
The circle was the heart thumping,
Her body was gold and yellow,
Everywhere I went she followed me.

Her fingers flowing from side to side,
The smell of roses,
She had a smile,
Her root was like the wind blowing.

The soil around the flower
Was the wrinkles on my body,
She shone at night.

Montanna Watson (10)
Highfields Primary School

The Tree

In autumn tears fall off the tree
The hands wave in the wind
The fingers tapping on windows
The eyes were sad as wind was blowing
The skin like an old lady's face.

Jennifer Taylor (11)
Highfields Primary School

Running

A green and light-blue day,
Smell of grass was cut,
Like fast barracuda swimming in the sea,
Touch of a sunny, windy day.

It was a glowing blustery day
And light-grey clouds in the sky,
I was green and black,
My heart was thumping.

Jonathan Timmins (10)
Highfields Primary School

THE DESERT

It was bare all throughout,
Dry skin scattered all around the Sahara landscape,
The mouth of the desert is now dried up,
The sun rises, shining on me.

I have to leave now,
Tears coming from my eyes,
They wetten the burning sand,
As I leave my footprints behind.

Hannah Pritchett (10)
Highfields Primary School

THE TREE

The arms on a tree blow,
Leaves blowing off the tree.
Fingers reaching to the sky.
Eyes watching me as I walk closer.
Its body standing straight and tall,
The hand was going side to side,
Waving to the one next door.

Kelliann Shakespeare (10)
Highfields Primary School

THE MAD COUPLE

(Objective: To write in the style as the same as The Highwayman)

The thunder of hooves and panting of breath,
The black masked face, promising death,
'Stand and deliver your money or your life.'
'Don't hurt me, but please take my wife,
She moans all the time, I want more,
Build that fire! Wash that floor!'
You could be my angel in disguise,
Shoot her now for a great big prize.'

'How could you say such a thing?'
'Kill him and I'll give you my ring,
My diamond tiara and all that's fine,
If your gun's not real, here use mine.'

'I don't want your gun or your money,
Something here feels really funny,
Be on your way before I change my mind,
How any married couple could be so unkind.'

'Come now woman, let's make haste
And forget the danger we just faced,
Don't look at me and start your chirping,
Just remember your husband is Dick Turpin.'

Matthew Highfield (11)
Highfields Primary School

TREES

Snowy arms waving in the wind,
The body standing in the garden,
Its eyes staring at me,
Its brown fingers swaying in the breeze.

The shiny silver ice sparkling in the glow,
It's so strong,
Just standing there,
Its fingers reaching to the stars.

Christopher Walker (10)
Highfields Primary School

THE LAKE

An elbow gently swaying,
Ripples walking,
It was blue, green, colour of shining,
It was bright,
It was like the yellow sunshine.

Beckoning me,
Cool water,
Tapping the side gently,
Full of silver sparkles,
A very glittering time.

The sun was smiling,
In the sparkling sky,
It was peaceful,
Very quiet.

The lake sparkled in the yellow sunshine,
The sun turned orange,
It went to sleep,
In came the breeze.

Liam Sellick (11)
Highfields Primary School

My Talent

Motorbike riding through the green fields,
Hitting a brick,
A human cannonball,
Flying through the clear air,
Landing on the hard brown ground.

My parents rushing me to hospital,
Trying to stay awake knowing I have concussion,
Seeing the red blood pouring out of my leg.

I had an x-ray,
The white flash hurting my eyes,
I was horrified,
Nothing was wrong,
The biggest shock of my life.

Ritchie Jones (10)
Highfields Primary School

A Past Memory Of A Cousin's Birth

Rushing to the hospital,
Hearing baby cry!
Smelling the fresh green countryside,
It's my golden delight.

I'm a sunshine raising
Light blues, oranges and yellows
Appearing in my head,
The spring trees blooming,
Lullabies singing.

Manpreet Bains (11)
Highfields Primary School

The Sun

Blonde hair shining in the sky
The finger reaching out to touch me
The heat of the sun fell down
It was orange fire

Blonde hair shining in the sky
It is glowing in the light blue world
Ideas for a new day
Growing in the mind

Blonde hair shining in the sky
Cotton wool up there too
Up there it is
Heaven!

Reanna Sherwood (10)
Highfields Primary School

The Flower

The first breath I take in the new world
Looking around seeing all the things.

My hands coming out of the ground,
Then my body is growing higher.

Looking up the cushioned blue and white sky,
Laughing and playing with my friends.

Finally growing old,
I can see the door of happiness,
Finally I'm free.

Charlotte Evans (11)
Highfields Primary School

Robber

The smell of winter,
Following me.
Robins singing their
Sweet songs.
Cold fog filling the house
Like a swarm of bees
To a flower.

My conscious screaming,
Like a madman.
It bangs and bangs
Inside me.
It said 'Stop' but I carried on
Walking down the stairs.

Brett Priest (11)
Highfields Primary School

Late October

Late October at 2pm,
My mind went blank,
As razors and needles went
Into my head.

Silver lighting struck,
It was dark, greens and blacks,
As I jumped head first,
On the crash mat in PE.

Christina Morton (10)
Highfields Primary School

My Mum

My heart was black,
Beating 100 times a second,
My face turned red with panic,
A tear trickled down my face.

I was full of sadness,
My heart was broken,
My vein turned purple,
She went blue.

Smelling of rotten fish,
Tasting of mouldy bread,
Her face turned blue,
She couldn't breathe.

Someone was tearing my heart with blades,
Another trickle of water slid down my face,
She was gone forever.

Luke Nicholls (10)
Highfields Primary School

Tree

I walked closer as its face looked back at me,
With a sparkle in its eyes
And its green hair blowing in the wind.

I walked closer and looked up,
As its arms reached out towards me,
Its fingers ready to pick me up
Like a baby in a cot.

Nicola Bircher (10)
Highfields Primary School

Trees

I ran to the bottom of the garden
To see them
Those lovely green fingers
And beautiful brown arms

I felt sorry
So sorry
It was all on its own
Just standing there
I know it's got life in it somewhere
It's just looking up at me
Looking up at me

They had brown skin
But soon they will be gone
Gone for good.

Stacey Keay (11)
Highfields Primary School

The Sea

The air is blowing the sea
Onto the wet, soft sand,
The heart of the sea
Beating on the side
Of a ship.

The waves are veins
Carrying the blood,
To break upon the rocks.

Shane Elliman (10)
Highfields Primary School

In The Early Morning Dew

In the early morning dew,
When the purples and reds leak across the sky,
When birds sing and ruffle their feathers
And the breeze flies by,

People are still in their comfy beds,
While the sun is rising
And the flowers nod their weary heads.

The cat twitches and waves his tail,
As the mouse scuttles by
And the rain drips off the woodland rail.

As the mist sways away
And the dew disappears
And the sun starts dancing to his regal day.

Hannah Detheridge (9)
Lutley Primary School

Excitement

The patched, painted pan was flying in the air,
As blue as the high sky,
It ran through the thin air.

A bouncy, bubbly, blue balloon blowing through the air,
It was as exciting as a roller coaster,
Butterflies tickling your tummy till it turns over.

I had no idea that the fire burns out,
The burner's like a dragon,
As big as a school playground.

James Workman (10)
Lutley Primary School

Hidden Treasure

Long ago in days of old
A treasure chest was full of gold
A ship set sail across the seas
The sails blowing gently in the breeze
All was calm or so they thought
The crew eating fish they had earlier caught
When suddenly without much warning
The weather changed like a lion roaring
The ship was thrown from left to right
The crew struggled hard all through the night
The ship, now battered, on the verge of sinking
The captain forced to do some serious thinking
Abandon ship! Or stay on board
The latter his crew could ill afford
Alas the harsh reality of the seas
Sent the water way above their knees
So from the lifeboat they looked on
The ship, so fine had simply gone
So to the graveyard of the deep
This trusted vessel laid to sleep
A ship that was once full of grace and pleasure
Now holds a host of hidden treasure!

Luke Johnson (8)
Lutley Primary School

In My Garden . . .

The flowers in my garden are blue and green,
The trees in my garden are growing supreme,
The grass in my garden is so green,
It really makes a beautiful scene,

The plants in my garden are so nice,
The little birds have a lovely voice,
The butterflies don't make any noise,
But there is plenty coming from the girls and boys.

Yasmin Siviter (9)
Lutley Primary School

SUMMERTIME

Summertime is the best time of the year
When new leaves grow and flowers appear
The start of the summer begins with the spring
Early in the morning the birds begin to sing
Pack away the winter clothes
Your coat, hat and scarf
Playing out in the garden
Sunshine makes me laugh
Going on picnics
Riding on my bike
Eating lots of ice cream
Doing things I like
Out in the garden in my paddling pool
Full of water to keep me cool
In summertime I stay up late
School is closed
This is great
Summertime means holidays, sun, sea and sand
Playing, swimming and laughing
Summertime is grand
Everything about the summer is fine
It doesn't last long, it soon becomes wintertime.

Chloe Robbins (8)
Lutley Primary School

See The Mistletoe

See the mistletoe,
Hung up high,
No more worries,
For needing to buy.

Christmas is here,
It's eventually come,
Everywhere you peer,
It's all full of fun!

So we've been grateful,
For this special season,
We all thank Jesus,
For being the reason

And then after that,
Where we have to wait,
Oh please again Santa . . .
And don't be late!

Harley Sargent-Farmer (10)
Lutley Primary School

My Puppies

Cheeky little puppies
Small, bouncy, black and brown
Heading for the garden
Where they run round and round

Getting under my feet
Chewing all they see
Digging holes all day long
Come running home for tea

My puppies are really cheeky
But they are lovely too
Although they can be naughty
I think they are just so . . . cute!

Ashleigh Wragg (8)
Lutley Primary School

A Cat's Life

Under the sun
On the garden path I lie
Ask me if I want to play
Miaow is my reply

Now I'm in the kitchen
Chasing a rat
Then curled up by the fire
Safe and sound I sat

In the garden
Chasing butterflies away
That's what all cats
Like to play

There's something all cats need
At the end of the day
A good sleep
After their play

Purrrrfect!

Charlotte Elwell (9)
Lutley Primary School

Barny Bug

One day when Barny Bug
Was walking up a tree,
He found himself staring at the sky,
He thought how could this be?

Barny asked a passing ant,
But all he got was a laugh
And then the very rude ant
Went prancing down the path.

He was puzzled for the answers,
Was he flying 'cause he'd grown wings
Or perhaps the world had suddenly turned round?
He knew there must be someone to tell him all those things.

Then his friend, Lily Spider came along the road,
Wearing a sparkly gown,
He asked if she knew the answer and was surprised when he got,
'Oh, silly Barny Bug, you're only upside down!'

Katie Slater (9)
Lutley Primary School

The Panic In A Balloon

Full of panic as my heart beat wildly,
I saw my birthday surprise,
A ride in the biggest air balloon in the world.
They swiftly sent me to the stairs
And I fearfully climbed in.
As my stomach shivered under my skin,
We flew through the air and gradually came down,
My stomach unwound.

Drew Saunders (10)
Lutley Primary School

WHAT AM I?

Deep down in a rocky cave,
There's something that never does behave,
Greeny-brown scaly skin,
Always makes a terrible din.
Jagged teeth,
Fiery breath,
Sometimes can cause instant death.
Zooming through the open sky,
You can see him raging by.
Booming roars, gaping jaws,
Leathery wings,
Frightening off kings.
Rather rude,
With a bad attitude.
What am I?

Guy Lewis (8)
Lutley Primary School

FEAR

I jumped into the basket full of people,
My heart was pounding,
But I knew I couldn't chicken out.
I was very fearful.
The clouds were as grey as cement.
My body went cold like an ice cube.
The balloon is a big sumo belly.

The brown, bumpy, basket flew away,
Gently dropped from the sky.

Kristopher Deeley (11)
Lutley Primary School

THE WAVE OF LIFE OR DEATH

The calm peaceful ocean is swaying
Back and forth
Making its way to a golden sanded beach
Taking who knows what with the flow of the tide
Suddenly from out of nowhere . . .
It appears
The rumble, the panic, silence
It's getting nearer
The pushing, shoving, crying, laughing fear

The twisting, turning bodies
The rush of water
The bubbles of breath escaping
Seeing a shimmer of life
Life or death.

Jackie Voss Wood (10)
Lutley Primary School

HUMAN SECRETS

Hidden in the mind
Amazing facts that can't be released
Memories that are never forgotten

Friendship relies on you, it surrounds your body
Fears are hidden in the heart
Secrets that can never be heard

The freedom of nature crawls everywhere
Nature is wonderful
Feelings and emotions that are bad and good.

Brandan Slater (7)
Mount Pleasant Primary School

The Snow Sparkles, The Snow Swirls

The snow sparkles, the snow swirls
Drifting slowly as it twirls
Falling silently to icy ground
Spiralling wildly round and round
And the snow sparkles, the snow swirls

The snow sparkles, the snow swirls
Snowflakes drift as the night sky whirls
Whistling rapidly like little girls
And the snow sparkles, the snow swirls

The snow sparkles, the snow swirls
Crumbling softly in little hurls
Glistening brightly above the clouds
Lots of people passing by, soon to be crowds
And the snow sparkles, the snow swirls.

Laura Harkin (9)
Mount Pleasant Primary School

Red Is For . . .

Red is for juicy berries that dangle from trees.
Red is for Santa's fluffy suit.
Red is for children's rosy red cheeks.
Red is for Rudolph's shiny nose leading the way with joy and pride.
Red is for baubles hanging elegantly from Christmas trees.
Red is for wrapping paper and presents too.

Lisa Henderson (9)
Mount Pleasant Primary School

The Four Seasons

Spring is when the winter wizard sleeps,
Among the slippy, muddy sleet.
Fresh and new, the animals are due,
To find some prey to eat.

Summer is when rabbits hop,
By the roasting sun,
People scorching, eating ice cream,
Also eating iced buns.
Water splashing all around,
By a sizzling beam that comes right down.

Autumn is when the leaves turn brown,
Some flowers hide their attractive faces,
Furry animals hide their winter feast,
In many secret places.
Flowers are sleeping so deeply,
As I watch, I tie my laces.

Winter is an arctic time, also so white,
The winter wizard ends his sleep,
Snowflakes are falling and bright,
The winter fox takes its first leap,
Lakes are like big ice lollies,
The snowman takes a peep.

Holly Taylor (10)
Mount Pleasant Primary School

Fireworks

Fireworks explode.
Fireworks flash.
Fireworks sparkle.
Fireworks whoosh.

Fireworks zigzag.
Fireworks screech.
Fireworks burst.
Fireworks do electric things!

Anthony Thomas (8)
Mount Pleasant Primary School

Seasons

The choking fog closing down on you,
Blizzards fiercely blasting cold wind down the street,
Icy patches ready to hurt.
Snow-troopers shooting snowballs in the snow,
Everything silent, only the whizzing sparrows concording
through the air.

Squalls of rain bouncing off the rooftops,
Breaks of strong sun.
Bakers baking bread and children come to see,
Lambs leaping happily,
A resilient fierce unconquerable winds catapult leaves flying high.

Whizzing wasps collecting,
Flowers sunbathing in the sun.
Honeybees racing to make honey,
Summery weather fills the sky,
Blazing fireball burns bark on trees.

Autumnal colour in the golden garden,
Scampering squirrels after nuts,
In the night glittering stars shine,
Plants turning white in the moonlight,
Leaves being hurled to the ground,
Cutting anything in their procedure.

Craig Hingley (10)
Mount Pleasant Primary School

THE SEASONS

When the flowers start to grow,
The silky grass begins to grow.
Lambs and sheep skip through the little breeze,
The waving things are the trees.
It will be an unstoppable sunny sky,
But it will eventually die.

Mistletoe hangs over your heads,
It looks like it is joined with little threads.
Animals are hibernating, there are none in sight,
They are sleeping, goodnight.
There is snow in the air,
It will get in your hair.

Crisp leaves fall,
Whilst people call.
Squirrels squirrel away their winter feast,
To keep them away from the horrid beasts.
It is very cold out there,
If you go out, it must be a dare.

Daffodils dance in the breeze
And so do the singing trees.
Scorching sun in the blazing sky,
I am very sure that this will not die.
Rabbits eat their fresh, fresh food,
The ants get in a very big mood.

Jemma Worsfold (10)
Mount Pleasant Primary School

HIDDEN TREASURE

Deep in the darkest jungle
Animals lurk around unseen in the air
The air smells like fresh water
Up above is the wonderful sky

God lives in Heaven
In the jungle there are snakes slithering on the ground
Frogs are jumping in the pond
The ground is full of seeds.

Hannah (8)
Mount Pleasant Primary School

THE YEAR

Refreshing breeze brushes past people,
The spring air whiffs up people's noses.
Mother Nature takes her turn,
The shrill croaking of grasshoppers lurking in the grass,
You can see daffodils when you pass.

Scorching weather comes from the ball of fire,
Aroma of golden luscious fruit.
Caterpillars snapping at the leaves,
The lightning lashing at the trees,
The pollen attaches to the bees.

Blustering weather of autumn,
Golden carpet covers the forest.
The moon shimmers in the sky.
The smell of sap oozing out of trees,
The autumn curse covers the country.

Ice polar weather,
Smell of berries crushed on the road.
Spectral frog covers the country.
A tornado catapults snow everywhere;
Thunder sounds like a grizzly bear.

Craig Hampton (11)
Mount Pleasant Primary School

THE SNOW SPARKLES, THE SNOW SWIRLS

The snow sparkles, the snow swirls,
Drifting slowly as it twirls,
Falling silently to icy ground,
Spiralling wildly round and round
And the snow sparkles, the snow swirls.

The snow sparkles, the snow swirls,
Snowflakes white look like pearls,
Falling silently down to the ground,
Like little girls running around
And the snow sparkles, the snow swirls.

The snow sparkles, the snow swirls,
Falling to the ground in little swirls,
White and frosty, bright and light,
Falling down from such a great height
And the snow sparkles, the snow swirls.

Sam Buxton (9)
Mount Pleasant Primary School

THE SNOW SPARKLES, THE SNOW SWIRLS

The snow sparkles, the snow swirls,
Drifting slowly as it twirls,
Falling silently on to the icy ground,
Spiralling wildly round and round
And the snow sparkles, the snow swirls.

The snow sparkles, the snow swirls,
Spiral flakes trapped in pearls,
Glistening white and icy cold,
Silver flakes holding gold
And the snow sparkles, the snow swirls.

Kittens racing like small girls,
Miaowing softly like a beauty curl,
Bright and frosty, shining white,
Falling silently in the night
And kittens racing like a pair of girls.

Abbie Bloomer (8)
Mount Pleasant Primary School

A Year Of Seasons In Months

The first month of the year is foggy and cold, as I,
By my mother and father were told.
Snowflakes and snow rule my world,
Which looks white and very cold!
I see hedgehogs hibernate,
In front of children as they shake.

This month is the start of spring,
When all the birds whistle and sing.
When all the flowers spurt from the ground,
Pansies show off their happy faces.

The next month gets really hot,
As if I'm sizzling in a pot.
The sun has fell down to Earth,
This is why I sweat.

I see squirrels hide their winter feast,
They have enough nuts to eat at least!
Trees are full of happy leaves,
Until the wind blows and they fall to the ground.

Shanna Guest (10)
Mount Pleasant Primary School

THE FOUR SEASONS

Spring brings torrential rain for dreadful April showers,
With occasional icy blasts;
A reminder of winter.
Lambs jogging in farms,
Scrumptious, delicious dark chocolate for Easter,
Fresh green leaves start to appear.

Summer brings the passionate sun,
The fierce sun roasts people like a roast steak.
Beach sand is an oven on high temperature,
A bit of torrential rain.
Shiny trees glitter while standing still,
Kids bombing into swimming pools to cool them down.

Autumn brings whirlwinds and gusts,
When golden crimson leaves drift to the ground.
The grass is jewelled into the colour of turquoise,
Busy bees are drunk from cider and start stinging people hour by hour.
Harvest food being gathered together,
Leaves rotting into brown and red.

Winter brings blasting blizzards,
Jack Frost turning the wood into crystal ice.
Silk on cobweb glitters in the trees,
Deer galloping in the freezing forest.
Holly and mistletoe shooting out of Christmassy houses,
Robins gliding out of snowy trees.

Christopher Hughes (10)
Mount Pleasant Primary School

SEASONS

The fleecy white lambs skip along
And beckon for the green grass to grow.
The blustery days sweep the dead leaves away,
To decorate our roads.
Plants are starting to mature again,
After a long winter sleep.

The summer brings a palette of colour,
Swaying in the breeze.
Deer prance across the high land,
Sneaky snakes slither slowly.
Cool breezes blow across the region,
Refreshing people here and there.

The blistering weather of summer has gone,
Autumn has brought back its chill.
Squirrels ready their winter store,
With nuts and berries.
A blast of vermilion, bronze and mauve,
Coming from the trees.

Snow comes down by the hour,
Making our world a motionless, colourless land.
Robins fly across the sky,
Down, down to the south.
Soon it will start to rain,
When this year starts again.

Owen Reese (10)
Mount Pleasant Primary School

SEASONS

Spring is upon us, the blossom is falling from the trees,
Sap is falling down the trees
And flowers are bursting into the moist soil.
Trees are reaching into the sky,
All little bugs are jumping into the sky.
Fish are swimming down the river, it is freezing cold.
The sky is blue and big clouds are floating in the air.

The sun is blazing in the air,
People are wearing shorts and T-shirts in the sun.
The sun's rays are making the land turn to brass.
A pomander of scents are all in the fields.

All the leaves are falling from all the trees,
Conkers are on all of the trees in the woods.
The sky is blue and green,
The clouds are drifting through the air,
The clouds are as fluffy as lambs,
The children are playing in the park by the woods.

All the little children are playing in the park
And making snowmen out in the snow
And making snowballs.
All the trees are white as snow
And the floor is white,
It is Christmas
And the rooftops are white.

Jamie Checketts (11)
Mount Pleasant Primary School

SEASONS

Summer has scorching weather,
People feeling heavier than a feather.
Little rabbits bouncing around,
Looking for food on the ground.
Flying through the air is water,
Bringing children away from watching slaughter.

Autumn brings the greyish fogs,
People are dreading to lose their dogs.
Grey bundles squirreling acorns away,
Readying their winter feast or they'll pay.
Leaves falling off the trees,
Flying in the little breeze.

Winter has a freezing gust,
Watching snow fall in the dust.
Animals in hibernation,
Sleeping through the snowy nation.
Snowballs flying through the air,
Children throwing when it's not fair.

In this weather there is hardly any sun,
Now the spring has just begun,
Little lambs charging around,
Worms hiding before they are found.
Flowers start to pop out of the ground,
In the breeze they sway around.

Daniel Meredith (10)
Mount Pleasant Primary School

THE FOUR SEASONS

Spring weather can be a bit of a pain,
Sometimes there's sun, sometimes there's rain.
Secretive squirrels search for food,
Newborn lambs hang out like dudes.
Flowers begin to appear,
The wind sounds like it's giving a cheer.

In the warmish, moving summer,
Now and then there's faint, loud thunder.
Racing rabbits race about
And the children love to shout.
Don't the flowers look so well,
These sorts of flowers begin to sell.

Autumn winds can be so frightening,
They like to howl, which makes them haunting.
Searching squirrels starve for treats,
Frightened foxes fight for meats.
The ground looks like a golden heaven,
Leaves come down seven by seven.

Winter weather has a gentle frost,
Trees are bare, their leaves are lost.
Happy hedgehogs hide in a ball,
Snowmen patrol their front lawns.
Teeth chattering, chilly snow,
People frozen head to toe.

Lucy Jones (11)
Mount Pleasant Primary School

The Seasons

Spring leads the tree,
When the winds start to flee,
Fresh leaves start coming,
Then the choir starts humming,
Rain and sun make rainbows,
Then the rivers start to flow.

Summer brings flowers that are bright,
The sun makes a gorgeous light,
Birds begin to sing,
Then the people start to fling,
The spicy sun sparkles in the sky,
When the birds begin to fly.

Autumn makes golden floors,
Then you can go outdoors,
Squirrels scurry away their nuts,
Animals hide in their beautiful huts,
The night turns dark,
Then everything turns to the park.

Winter brings the crystal view,
Then the animals have a clue,
People start to play on the lake,
Snow then begins to flake,
Robins start to appear
And don't forget the great deer.

Nathan Lewis Farmer (11)
Mount Pleasant Primary School

FOUR SEASONS

A flushed season where plants start to grow,
We've got past the icy season of snow.
A shrill breeze whistles in my ear,
Insects come back without any fear.
Birds advance home and blissfully sing,
The season I love is the joyful spring!

A scorching season where flowers are born from grass,
With the sun shining brightly the land turns to brass.
Honeybees keep dancing in the radiant light;
The sun is a spotlight, it is such a sight.
This season is better than any other,
The best season of course is the radiant summer!

A drizzly season where the weather is bleak,
People with chilly hands, warm clothes they seek.
Leaves change to appealing colours,
This season's more beautiful than any others.
The cool damp weather is out to haunt 'em,
Only joking, the season's only autumn!

A spiritless season where the ground is white,
The floor's always like that, even at night.
Unblemished snow relaxing on the ground,
The snow will stay a long time without a single sound.
The horrible wind hurts like a sharp splinter,
But I still love the season and it's called winter!

Danielle Smith (10)
Mount Pleasant Primary School

SEASONS

Spring is a wonderful thing,
At you the weather does sing.
Daffodil and the smallest flower,
Seem to just overpower.
The chicks are safe in mother's case,
While the farmer ties his lace

From above the blazing sun burns,
As the Earth slowly turns.
The wonderful smell of the sweet orchid,
Then comes off the honey lid.
Shooting water in the street,
Children come and go like sleet.

The falling leaves make a crimson floor,
High above birds do soar.
The tallest trees look like stone,
Hallowe'eners do so moan.
A bird is seen flying south,
While insects are caught in its mouth.

Across the road spread is grit,
Then the fires are lit.
Winter brings the drab downpours
And above no bird soars.
With no sun to give them power,
Oft' dies the wonderful flower.

Daniel Homer (11)
Mount Pleasant Primary School

THE SEASONS

In comes the rushing, rolling rivulet of rain,
The sun begins to weaken again.
The plants begin to blossom and bloom,
As the ants start to come, we are all in doom.
All the dogs are being invaded,
Lots of fleas are making their fur become faded.

The sun is cooking all the flowers and turning them to toast,
It is again being called a fireball and now is starting to boast.
The plants and trees are beginning to sweat,
All the butterflies are appearing in nets.
Lots of dogs run after balls,
People trip over them and fall.

In comes the fog confusing everyone who comes out the mall,
The sun is turning very small.
Conkers defect inside their sharp thorny cases.
All the bugs are constructing bases.
Lots of dogs chase after balls,
All the owners start to call.

The snow sneaks softly down onto the ground.
The sun transmogrifies into an ice cube that is stern and round.
The plants are turning a rusty brown,
All the bugs who live in the trees are trying to dig down and down.
All the pets have to come indoors,
So there are plenty of hairs all over the floors!

Amanda Tomkins (10)
Mount Pleasant Primary School

The Seasons

In this month the fields are green,
There are no rain clouds to be seen.
The snow and snowmen disappear
And the rivers and lakes are crystal clear.
Daffodils and daises roam the land,
As pollen dust falls into my hand.

In this month foxes scurry across the roads,
As leaves appear on the trees in loads.
Cloudless skies above your head;
Make you want to curl up in bed.
The sun is shining, burning the ground,
Making ants and spiders yell like a hound.

In this month squirrels and other beasts,
Hide away their winter feasts.
The beautiful flowers wilt and die,
As the sun is distinguished, high up in the sky.
An impenetrable fog barring you from your hope,
Like a fluffy heap of liquid soap.

In this month mistletoe appear on the ceiling above
And underneath kisses the symbols of love.
Fierce winds scream at you,
As drops of hail fall into my shoe.
A blanket of ice spreads itself over the world,
As cannonballs of snow are hurled.

Amanda Rose (10)
Mount Pleasant Primary School

SECRETS OF NATURE

Deep down in the forest,
Caterpillar changes to cocoon,
From a tiny cocoon to an amazing moth,
Spreading its beautiful wings.

As your greatest desires overcome your worst fears,
You will start to realise that
You can stand up to them.

From the heartbeat of an animal,
To the heartbeat of a human,
Anything that lives should be left in peace.

Ben Carrington (8)
Mount Pleasant Primary School

NEW YEAR

R eaching the new things in the world
E veryone should care for each other
S top people from doing bad things to the world
O pen the future and leave the past
L eave no one alone, help them be happy in the New Year
U nlock the pieces in the world
T reat people to food and drink to help them have a happy life
I 'll try to work and enjoy the things I do
O pen your hope and have a better life than you've had before
N ew things will happen, I will make this year an exciting one.

Haydn Bennett (9)
Mount Pleasant Primary School

NEW YEAR

R esolutions are things to remember to achieve and not to forget.
E very day is easy if it is good but you need to learn from bad days.
S anctions are hated, rewards are loved, but people can change that,
by caring and sharing.
O nly the sad memories are hard to forget but good must
remain in your heart.
L ove is too special to be wasted, resolutions are something to keep.
U ncover lost memories of long, long ago, try to recover good things.
T his year will be one to remember, so make sure you
focus your efforts.
I f our world is not looked after then we all will be lost.
O nly the New Year will bring joy and happiness.
N ever forget the New Year, the happiness, the celebrations,
the memories and the new chance.

Jordan Madkins (9)
Mount Pleasant Primary School

LIFECYCLES

Caterpillars biting chunks out of leaves,
Then releasing into a butterfly that flutters,
With its multicoloured wings with wonderful colours.

Flying to find a place which is fun,
To lay eggs, to start the cycle again,
So there's more life.

Eggs crack into a caterpillar,
Crawling to find a place to release into a butterfly,
Beginning again.

Emma Garbett (7)
Mount Pleasant Primary School

The Mind

The mind holds many secrets
Never to be known
Never to be seen

The mind can escape anything
But you will never know it

The mind roams deep into the jungle
Awaiting the jungle king

The mind will escape all your fears
Your mind will always be your friend

The mind can bring happiness and sadness
In all and every way.

Katie Woodbine (7)
Mount Pleasant Primary School

Hidden Treasure

There is love in your heart when you need it,
There are treasures and secrets too
Your heart is a special place to be
And it is a wonderful feeling too
The beating of the heart is like a comforting blanket
It is soft and warm and a wonderful feeling too
We curl up together the two of us
Me and this heart of mine.

Stevie-Leigh Hyde (7)
Mount Pleasant Primary School

NEW YEAR

R esolutions are a chance to start a brand new life and leave
  the bad things behind us.
E verybody's bad memories can make tears in your eyes.
S ome are emotional, some are joyful.
O pen a clean piece of paper and start again.
L earn knowledgeable skills and you will become clever.
U nderstand the New Year is an opportunity to celebrate.
T hink and you will enjoy your New Year's resolution.
I really like my resolution.
O ther people enjoy their New Year, celebrating the good times.
N ew Year is a brilliant time to make your life change.

Claire Hampton (9)
Mount Pleasant Primary School

SILVER IS . . .

Silver is glistening snowflakes.
Silver is fluffy snow.
Silver is icy icicles.
Silver is fluttering angels.
Silver is flickering stars.
Silver is the lovely silver skis of Santa's sleigh.
Silver is the itchy tinsel.
Silver is Frosty the snowman.
Silver is the glittery glitter on Christmas cards.
Silver is the glistening silver frost.

Rebecca Johnson (8)
Mount Pleasant Primary School

The Snow Sparkles, The Snow Swirls

The snow sparkles and the snow swirls,
The snow sparkles, the snow swirls,
Drifting slowly as it twirls,
Falling silently to the icy ground,
Spiralling wildly round and round
And the snow sparkles and the snow swirls.

Looking like glistening sparkling pearls,
Some Christmas trees glitter and shine.
Lighting up a happy Christmas time
And the snow sparkles and the snow swirls.

No more swirling, drifting twirls,
The snow begins to drip and melt,
The snowman's left with just a belt,
The snow sparkles and the snow swirls.

Daniel Such (8)
Mount Pleasant Primary School

Hidden Feelings

Dreams float, amazing facts come,
Like a smile of a crescent moon,
Wishes are in the head.

Fears hide but do evolve,
Like someone who never had harm done,
Happiness and emotions are in their heart.

Hidden behind those clouds are gods,
Gods like the sun shining,
Guardian angels help with feelings.

Bethany Madkins (8)
Mount Pleasant Primary School

Sea Secrets

Lower than the depths of the sea,
Under the ticklish sand,
Sparkling keys that are discovered by huge crabs,
A box of sparkles with coins of worthy gold.

Dolphins do have feelings,
Love comes from their heart,
It's cruel for horrid fishermen
To kill all that precious love.

Deep down in those splashes,
Magical things could fly,
For many hidden treasures
Are hidden in the sea!

Georgia Rose Williams (8)
Mount Pleasant Primary School

The Colour Of Winter

White is the colour of winter.
White is like sharp, long, pointy icicles.
White is round snowmen being built.
White is the colour of swirling snowflakes
Falling softly from the sky.
White is like the smooth, round snow.
White is beautiful snow falling onto the ground.
White is the cold frost making children's cheeks glow red.
White is the colour of winter.

Rebecca Beresford (9)
Mount Pleasant Primary School

New Year

R esolutions are the chance to begin a change of life.
E veryone gets the chance to have a fabulous time
and make excellent decisions.
S ome celebrations for New Year are very fun and exciting.
O pportunites are very useful for you and others.
L ife can change when you have a resolution.
U se your resolution to help you in your life.
T ime to remember the good and learn from the bad times
from the last year.
I mportant things can happen when you make a resolution.
O pportunities should be used and not left on paper.
N ew Year is the time to celebrate, so come along and join the party.

Jodie Cox (9)
Mount Pleasant Primary School

Heart's Love

H eart hides love and emotions
E at away the horrible moments
A t the right time let your feelings
R un loose
T ears have fears
S ecrets you don't want to tell

L ove lies inside the heart
O bjection turns away
V ases hold friendship
E motions give a smile.

Bethany Hyde (8)
Mount Pleasant Primary School

THE SNOW SPARKLES, THE SNOW SWIRLS

The snow sparkles, the snow swirls,
Drifting slowly as it twirls,
Falling silently to icy ground,
Spiralling wildly round and round
And the snow sparkles, the snow swirls.

The snow sparkles, the snow swirls,
Like dancers dancing, then doing twirls,
The snowflakes mounding like a flower
And when you taste it, it's always sour,
Then the snow sparkles, the snow swirls.

The snow sparkles, the snow swirls,
When squirrels turning and doing curls,
The snow all crispy
And looks like whisky,
The snow sparkles, the snow swirls.

Andrew Taylor (9)
Mount Pleasant Primary School

HIDDEN INSIDE YOU

Hidden inside you,
Blood surrounds the heart,
Keeping the friendship in.

The heart tries to
Keep the blood flowing.

Happiness keeps the heart
Going round and round.

Daniel Foster (8)
Mount Pleasant Primary School

THE SENSATIONAL SEASONS

Blasting blizzards blow the leaves around,
Racket of thunder makes a sound.
Foggy days, foggy nights,
Block out the wonderful sights.

Lambs leap on the land,
Gathering flowers in our hand.
Pleasant rainbows start to appear,
The fox's rivals are in fear.

Skipping squirrels lurk all day,
Seeing children work and play.
Floating leaves which float in the air,
Howling wind moves everywhere.

Roasting heat ball stalks the land,
Sweaty people drag their bodies around,
Buzzing bees buzz around,
Unhappy schools are out of bounds.

James Taylor (10)
Mount Pleasant Primary School

LOST LOVE

Love is hidden in a little corner in a little heart,
Sometimes love comes out of fears, awaiting to be seen.
Friendship shows as you play with your friends,
Singing songs in your heart, dancing happily.
Secrets hide as you don't say your worries and your fears,
Hide in a little corner,
Deep, deep inside you.

Katie North (8)
Mount Pleasant Primary School

THE ROMAN BATTLE

The battle started, the Celts and Romans were fighting.
The Roman's shield was blazing off a sword, sparks were flying out.
Their helmets were getting scratched.
His sword with fiery blades missed attacking the Celt's.
The Roman's javelin frightened the Celt, then withdrew it.
You could see his armour glisten like the moon.
The Roman got his dagger out, the Celt fell over.
The Roman tried to stab him but the Celt jumped over.
The Celt jabbed and shone his shield like gold.
The Roman threw his javelin but hit the shield.
The Roman distracted the Celt and picked up his javelin.
The Roman got his sword out and stabbed the Celt.

Matthew Mifsud (8)
Mount Pleasant Primary School

HIDDEN TREASURES OF NATURE

Deep at the bottom of the ocean
There is a cavern
Like a bottomless pit
Jewels protected by shipwrecks

High above the stars
Heaven hidden from sight
Like a sea made from clouds

Protected from sight
Animals lurk - for their prey
Like wounded soldiers they hunt.

Brett Smith (8)
Mount Pleasant Primary School

THE SNOW SPARKLES, THE SNOW SWIRLS

The snow sparkles, the snow swirls
Drifting slowly as it twirls
Falling silently to the icy ground
And the snow sparkles, the snow swirls

The snow sparkles, the snow swirls
As the snowmen look at girls
Standing in a field so cold
Snowflakes falling look like gold
And the snow sparkles, the snow swirls

The snow sparkles, the snow swirls
Looking like big fat curls
These snowflakes cannot hear sound
They swirl down and touch the ground
And the snow sparkles, the snow swirls.

Lauren Hadley (9)
Mount Pleasant Primary School

THE DEEPEST OCEAN

Deep down in the deepest sea
Is a sunken ship.
Glittering gold that nobody has seen before,
The ship is a chocolate colour.

At the top of the deepest ocean,
As the seagulls dive and eat fish,
The seagulls splash in the ocean,
The sun.

Lydia Bennett (7)
Mount Pleasant Primary School

Hidden Treasure

A small seed is deep under the dark ground,
Waiting like a starving animal to be fed,
Flowers are facing the shining sun.

Flaming fire flashes by with sparkles in it,
Lava is bubbling out of the bursting volcano,
Flowing into the valley.

Inside a tiny cocoon, a caterpillar
Charges into a beautiful, brilliant butterfly.

Deep down in the heart of a human is friendship,
Friendship flows around the delicate bodies of us all,
Then it suddenly bursts out of the heart of friendship.

Simone Round (8)
Mount Pleasant Primary School

White Is . . .

White is icicles hanging up on the roof.
White is snowflakes falling silently to the ground.
White is soft snow on Christmas Day.
White is cuddly, little polar bears just been born.
White is the Arctic fox hunting for food.
White is Arctic in the icy ground.
White is Antarctic with skiing penguins sliding on the ice.
White is frost in the freezing winter.
White is misty fog in the icy winter.
White is fluffy snowmen walking in the air.
Christmas is here!

Emma Paynter (9)
Mount Pleasant Primary School

LOVE

Love in your heart is the best thing in the world
Your wishes come true and your love for your family

Feelings you get for your husband and your mum and dad
And if you have got children

Also you have feelings for some of your friends.

Daniel Appleton (7)
Mount Pleasant Primary School

GOLD

Gold tinsel like the sparkle of the gold moonlight.
Gold sleigh bells like the bells of the church ringing.
Gold baubles like the hotness of the sun.
Gold rings like the crusty leaves.
Gold chocolate money like the goldness of some rings.

Thomas Ashley Wilkins (9)
Mount Pleasant Primary School

HEART OF A CATERPILLAR

Deep in the hidden heart of the caterpillar
Hides its fear and love
Dreaming of the flying life of a butterfly
While it's squashed into its cocoon.

Todd Millward (8)
Mount Pleasant Primary School

Hidden Treasure

Deep in your heart lies love
Like the love for your family
You care for everyone

High in Heaven lies God
Like fluffy clouds in the sky
You can see angels playing harps

Down in the sea mermaids combing their hair
With beautiful colours on their tails

In the jungles lions creeping behind bushes
To leap on prey, slithering snakes hissing
Stripy tigers roaring.

Kate Wills Adams (8)
Mount Pleasant Primary School

New Year

R emember the good things from the year before.
E njoy the new things even more.
S ay good things to mend people's hearts.
O nly you can make a difference in your heart.
L ive safely in this dangerous world.
U nder the bad, there's always good.
T eardrops are shared throughout this world.
I n the New Year we have a chance to start something new.
O ver the rainbow we go to remember the fun things.
N ow the year's just begun, so make a resolution, everybody can.

Kirsty Cave (10)
Mount Pleasant Primary School

NEW YEAR

R eady for a fresh start every year.
E verybody does better every year.
S o many fresh starts are made in New Year.
O ld is forgotten every year round.
L ook to the new not the old times.
U seful things will happen in many years to come.
T ake an opportunity to do better in the world.
I n New Year everybody should be celebrating.
O pportunities for a fresh start await you.
N ew Year is about getting together, being safe in our world
for many years to come.

Kristopher Fellows (9)
Mount Pleasant Primary School

NATURE

High in the bright forest,
Like stars the trees sparkle,
Unknown animals move about in happiness.

Branches of trees are in surprise,
Like decorations, cocoons hang,
In the cocoons butterflies wait to be free.

Deep in the pond little eggs wait to be hatched,
Little tadpoles jump out and swim around the pond all day,
They are happy for their freedom.

Tiffany Johnstone (7)
Mount Pleasant Primary School

NEW YEAR

R eady to make a new, exciting year
E verybody can turn over a new leaf
and make the New Year much better
S tart a brilliant year achieving new things
O nly you can make new adventures
to explore in the world
L eave all the memories of the last year behind
and create new ones in the New Year
U nfold new challenges to complete through the year
T ry to forget all the difficulties in the year
I t's hard to stick to a new year's resolution
O pportunities to improve in the year
N ew Year is a chance to create a new life.

Charlotte Stokes (10)
Mount Pleasant Primary School

NEW YEAR

R ewinding to the rotten years and just simply forget about them.
E veryone has to have a good memory from the early years
that have gone by.
S hining lights are at the end of the tunnel.
O ur minds are filled with memories from the past,
some wicked, some pleasing.
L oving memories that we recall to be admired.
U npleasant people disappear from our minds.
T hings will look up in the future, so don't be upset.
I gnorant times won't happen if you focus on the future.
O pportunities are opening out in front of us.
N ew Year resolutions should be made and stuck to.

Laura Banks (10)
Mount Pleasant Primary School

NEW YEAR

R eady for a new start.
E ven with yourself.
S o come along and join the party with everybody else.
O h what a great day for going out.
L et's look at the past and see how we have done.
U nknown things you discover can be something to do with New Year.
T he winter days are great for fun.
I n the New Year you have the chance to change.
O n the day before New Year, you are so excited to see
  what your resolution is.
N ew Year is a perfect time for resolution.

Lewis Greensall (9)
Mount Pleasant Primary School

THE MUMMY

As the mummy rises from the chamber
It breaks the curse of the tomb

Then he walks deep into the jungle
Snakes slither up its crispy body and drop out of him

Then he walks back to the creepy tomb
And gets back into the cage to be buried under the sand again.

Joshua Lambe (8)
Mount Pleasant Primary School

Hidden Treasure

Love is down in your heart
Wishes are drawn in your mind
Fears are hidden inside your heart

There is a small seed on the ground
Happiness and amazing facts are down inside your mind
Caterpillars hopping off the leaves
Badgers are digging on the ground

The seed grows in the ground
Flowers facing the sun
The sun shining down on them
The sky is making fresh air.

Jasmine Worsfold (8)
Mount Pleasant Primary School

New Year

R esolutions are very good.
E vents are good and sometimes are not.
S ome people make mistakes in their work.
O ur world is full of people.
L ives might change at New Year.
U nderstand the year when it goes.
T hey believe the old year goes by.
I n the New Year everything changes.
O nce New Year comes, New Year stays
N ew Year is great when it comes.

Robert Bloomer (9)
Mount Pleasant Primary School

SPRING

A new beginning is upon the Earth,
We celebrate new life and miracles of birth.

Sap is rising from the warm moist ground,
Buds are bursting, fresh fragrance surrounds.

Fluffy bundles friskily frolicking across the meadow,
Where new lush green grass and flowers grow.

Kieran Russell (10)
Mount Pleasant Primary School

HIDDEN TREASURE

There is a seed wanting to be fed,
So it can grow.
It is waiting to grow into a sunflower,
It has just popped out of a seed.
In a heart there is love hidden inside,
Secrets are very special, we keep them inside.

Amie Adams (7)
Mount Pleasant Primary School

THE SEASONS

A new beginning is upon the Earth,
We celebrate new life and the miracle of birth.
Sap is rising from the warm moist ground,
Buds are bursting, fresh fragrance surround.
Fluffy bundles frisky frolicking across the meadow,
Where new lush green grass and flowers grow.

Samantha Stanyard (11)
Mount Pleasant Primary School

Spring

A new beginning is upon the Earth,
We celebrate new life and the miracle of birth.
Sap is rising from the warm, moist ground,
Buds are bursting, fresh fragrance surround.
Fluffy bundles friskily, frolicking across the meadow,
Where now lush green grass and flowers grow.

Paul Godwin (10)
Mount Pleasant Primary School

Hidden Treasures

A caterpillar hidden in a cocoon comes out
And turns into a beautiful butterfly
Blue, red, yellow, green, white, black, pink
And sky blue colours that were hidden inside
Stand out and sparkle and glow in the shining sunlight.

Leah Bangham (7)
Mount Pleasant Primary School

Nature

Deep in the darkest jungle
You see a seed that turns amazingly into a big tree
High in the blue and emerald sky
Is the enormous white mountain top
Beautiful clouds hide Heaven
And the wonderful God.

Amie Dingley (7)
Mount Pleasant Primary School

HIDDEN TREASURE

Deep in the darkest underground cavern,
Lurk crystals like the moon shining,
People digging for shiny stones and pebbles.

Up high, the birds swoop overhead
And grab worms and fish to give to their young,
They glide in warm, breezy air.

Up in the Siberian treetops live monkeys,
Full of life,
The monkeys live with insects, grapes and snakes.

Ryan North (8)
Mount Pleasant Primary School

HIDDEN TREASURES

Deep in the loving heart
Like a big bass drum beating away
Is a place with lots of secrets

High above in the azure blue sky
The clouds are fluffy like candyfloss
Sun blazing brightly

Captured in the middle of your mind are the things you don't know
Like wishes that you always wanted to come true
A dream hides there.

Philippa Coley (7)
Mount Pleasant Primary School

SEASONS

Winter brings sparkling frost,
Wander off and you will get lost.
Clouds black as coal,
As a stormy deluge keeps us cold.
Fog scatters on your windscreen,
As we pass the world unseen.

Golden, scorching sun,
Baking apples ready to eat.
Oppressive summer,
Makes us reach.
Heatwaves coming time to time,
Ice creams melting all the time.

Leaves fluttering from trees,
Like a blanket covering everything.
Everything's cool;
Everything's calm.
Also icicle rain,
Makes us go in our home again.

A gust of wind
Blows us down.
Cyclone winds race past,
Even though it comes last.
Creamy pink apple blossom
Bursting from the buds.

Lewis Mason (10)
Mount Pleasant Primary School

My Sister

No matter where we go or what we do,
Sister's in the loo.
It doesn't matter if we're late for an important date,
Sister's in the loo.

What does she do in there?
Maybe she's squeezing another spot,
Or checking the parting in her hair.
Doesn't matter, sister's in the loo.

Maybe she's a secret agent undercover
And she's bugged the loo roll.
Or maybe she's just sitting on the loo.
Doesn't matter, sister's in the loo.

Sometimes I think she secretly reads my Beano in there,
You never know, she could be a Dennis fan.
All I know is if we're going out,
Sister's in the loo.

She says it's nerves,
I don't think so.
But it's a mystery we'll never solve,
All I know is, sister's in the loo!

Robert Tromans (10)
Peter's Hill Primary School

View Of A Car

A swift mover
A bashed bumper
A burning rubber
A polished shimmer

A blasting player
An angry driver
A revving engine
A speeding motorist.

Nicola Homer (11)
Peter's Hill Primary School

MY DOG

I have a little dog,
Poppy is her name,
She thinks she is a little frog,
But she is rather tame.

She sits on the window sill,
Then she barks and barks some more,
At everyone going past,
They get quite a shock,
Because she's ever so small.

Upon the landing,
She chews her chew sticks,
They stink the house out,
But they don't care,
Even if we do.

The kitchen drawer opens,
The lead comes out,
She gets all excited,
Because she knows she's going out,
With other dogs she runs and plays,
Either way, she doesn't mind.

Abbie Wilkins (11)
Peter's Hill Primary School

My Witchy, Flying, Weirdo Sis!

Does your sister always invade
Your room, your toys, it's a barricade!
You tell your mum and dear old dad,
Couldn't care less, it's really sad!

Next she heads over to your chest of drawers,
Where your secret diary is, 'That's mine, not yours.'
And when you try and pull her back,
She laughs then gives me a whooping *smack!*

You tell your mum and dear old dad,
They couldn't care less, it's really sad!

So I wandered into Sissy's room,
Where I stumbled on her witch's broom.
Tall and dark and primed for flight,
(She hadn't used it yet that night.)

She used it when the moon was small,
For popping down the village hall.
Where once a month if she got the chance,
She grooved on down at the local dance!

I don't know if Mum's aware of this,
My witchy, flying, weirdo sis
And if she's not, should I tell?
Then risk a get your own back spell!

Tom Holdaway (10)
Peter's Hill Primary School

View Of A Parent

A noisy snorer
A good cooker
A quiet reader
A big drinker

A constant sleeper
A piggish eater
A mouse hater
A cat lover.

Matthew Page (10)
Peter's Hill Primary School

What Happens In The Staffroom

Mrs West makes the coffee,
Then realises there is no tea.
By this time she is stroppy,
Not to mention stressed and bossy.

Mr Rook stands on a chair,
Trying to stop himself from going spare.
He has had enough kids for one day,
Well one and a half hours anyway.

Miss New sits down being very calm,
She looks at her fingertips and then her palm.
Begins to examine the curved lines,
Looking for marriage signs.

Mrs Hagley wonders about having some tea,
Then realises she's lost her classroom key.
It's the second time this week,
Must be her unlucky streak.

Mr Spee dreamed of when he would get his pay,
Ping! Bell's gone, end of play.
What happens in the staffroom?
What do the teachers do?

Erin Gilhooley (10)
Peter's Hill Primary School

The Castle Across The Sea

On an island
Across the sea
There's a large, dark castle
Staring down at me.

It's tall and old
And it's crumbling down,
As the sun sets behind it,
It looks like a crown.

There are two large towers
Standing very tall
And all around the castle,
A strong brick wall.

The castle was untouched
For many, many years,
Until one stormy night,
When I travelled there with fears.

I found myself a boat
And I sailed across the sea,
I rowed to that old castle
Staring down at me.

I boldly stood
In front of the door,
There were thistles all around
And brambles on the floor.

I slowly crept inside,
Then I suddenly felt colder,
When a thin, bony hand
Gripped me on the shoulder.

I looked up in fright and what did I see?
Two dark, scary eyes staring down at me.

Robyn Gillard (10)
Peter's Hill Primary School

SISTER, SISTER

Little step, little step
Little step nearer
Crept the two hundredth
'Forward the girl brigade
Ravage her secrets' she said

'Quick, she's coming' she said
'Hide before you're found' she cried
I ran down the stairs, not seeing anyone
'The coast is clear' she said
She crept into my room

I ran up the stairs
Heard rustling in my room
I wondered who it was and crept upon my own room
I knocked my sister over
She started crying
'Stop, stop, stop it' she said
My mum stormed upstairs and put us in our rooms
I never ever left my room again.

Natalie Bishop (11)
Peter's Hill Primary School

CALAMITY KID

Oh fiddly-de
Sir is going to be mad at me
No! My alarm didn't go off
And all my books have been put up the loft
Oh how I wish this was a dream!

Here down the stairs I fall
Now I've ripped my coat upon the wall
From in the kitchen came a call
As I stumbled in the hall
Oh how I wish this was a dream!

As I tumbled down the road
Thinking of my locker code
I wondered if Sir would go mad
And whether he'd say I'm a naughty lad
Oh how I wish this was a dream!

When I finally got to school
I fell into the fountain's pool
Pinch me someone, just to see if I'm asleep
Through two little slits I did peep
Oh bless my soul it *was* a dream!

Amy Southall (10)
Peter's Hill Primary School

DAVID BECKHAM

There's only one more game to go,
Don't score Greeks, no, no, no,
We played so well over the last few weeks,
We better win those foreign Greeks,
Help us now the Greeks have scored,
No, no, no, the English roared,

It's the last minute in the game,
We're going to lose, it's such a shame,
Time's running out as the seconds tick,
Yes, Beckham's got a free kick,
We watch the ball go up and up,
Beckham scores, we're in the World Cup.

Robin Smith (11)
Peter's Hill Primary School

MY HERO

My hero doesn't save the world,
My hero doesn't fly,
My hero doesn't put out fires
And I'll tell you why.

My hero hasn't got a cape
Or a suit or tights,
My hero lives on Earth,
Right by my side.

My hero isn't famous
And known around the world,
My hero isn't in the papers
And on TV shows.

In fact my hero
Is the one who made me,
The best person in the world,
Would have to be . . .
Julie! My mum,
She's my hero, that's for sure!

Benjamin Taylor (11)
Peter's Hill Primary School

THE JEWEL

A falling star, the sea, the moon,
It's going to hit the Earth, is it too soon?
A lonely child, alone and afraid.

The boy looks up, dismayed,
He hides behind a rock alone and afraid.

The star hits, bright sparks flicker,
It lands quite near the boy.

Inside the star was a bright gold jewel,
It cost about the same as twelve swimming pools.

The boy got up and edged towards the star,
He suddenly stopped and stood like a bar.

He sits and stares,
He sees white mares,
Riding across the clouds.

He wishes he could show his family,
But sadly he has none.

But then his mind goes blank
And his hopes sank.

He was found by the army in a tank.

Jon Worton (10)
Peter's Hill Primary School

VIEW OF A CAT

A fuzz ball
A sly seeker
A fur coat
A fishy animal

A noisy thing
A trouble maker
A fish eater
A super sleeper.

John-Luke Stephens (10)
Peter's Hill Primary School

VIEW OF A SQUIRREL

A swift speeder
A tree climber
An acorn eater
A nut storer
A fur ball
A tree jumper
A soft mover
A non-flyer.

David Bayley (10)
Peter's Hill Primary School

VIEW OF A DOG

A deafening barker,
A good listener,
A winning animal,
A big biter,
A fast runner,
A playful obeyer,
A fun player,
A toy destroyer.

Charlotte Woodall (11)
Peter's Hill Primary School

I WISH

'Mum, Tim's nicked my homework.'
'Now you listen to me young lady, how can a little three year old boy do such a horrid thing, he couldn't, so don't blame him, now go to your room.'

Slam.
Now I will have to do my homework all over again,
Now where is that diary, ah, here it is.
Mum is always blaming me for everything, I just wish . . .

Dear Diary,
I thought it would be great to have a little brother,
But Tim, well Tim is the worst brother anyone could have.
I wish I could be away from Tim, Mum and Dad and well, this place.
I wish I could be away from school,
Away from Amy, Vicki and Abbey the show-offs.

I wish . . . I wish I could be on a
. . . unicorn flying across the sky,
Jumping from marshmallow cloud to cloud,
Watching its white mane swish in the wind.

I wish . . . I could live in a
. . . forest full of strawberries and nuts,
I would eat them for breakfast, lunch and dinner,
I would eat them with a squirrel.

I wish . . . I could have fun . . . underwater
With dolphins and seahorses,
But I'd stay away from the sharks,
I'd swim, toss and turn, day in, day out.

I wish, I wish . . . I wish,
'Ellie it's teatime.'
Maybe I will wish another day.

Jade Oakley (10)
Peter's Hill Primary School

The Witch That Haunts The School

Horrid chants
Ugly hair
She flies the broom
Upon the stair

Pointy nails
Puppy-dog tails
Without this her
Power would fail

All the horror's
Just begun
Now there's no time
To have great fun

Endless screams
Thumping hearts
Awful nights before school starts

Tigers snarl, giants roar
Just one of the chants all before school
The stare upon that fearsome face
Could blow you into outer space

Grey, dark
Warts and all
That's the witch that haunts the school

Snake's tongue
Blood everywhere
I still had to stand and stare

So if you want to stay on the right side
Don't ever come to Westside.

Hannah Griffiths (10)
Peter's Hill Primary School

WHERE DO TEACHERS KEEP THEIR PETS?

Mrs Mare has a rat in her hair.
Mr Screw keeps his gerbil in the loo.
Mrs Mimms, her dog's in the bins.
Mrs War's tortoise lives in the stores.

That is strange, but wait there's more:-

The cats behind the door belong to Mr Law.
The spiders in the attic belong to Mrs Batty.
Then of course there's the bats, we can't forget those,
The scary black bats belong to delicate Miss Rose.

Now that's not all, there's still some more:-

Mr Reed's iguana lives in a drawer.
The caretaker's fish, in a tank you would think, but not in our school,
They live in the sink.
All this in a school, yes it is true,
But in my opinion, it's more like a zoo.

Joshua Hughes (11)
Peter's Hill Primary School

A VIEW OF A MOUSE

A silent creeper,
A cheese nibbler,
A tiny biter,
A food stealer,
A hole lover,
A cat's dinner,
An unusual customer,
A small whisper.

Sarah Grove (10)
Peter's Hill Primary School

Treasure Island

Deep in the caves
Of a faraway land,
Is a great pile of treasure,
Buried under the sand.

Glittering rubies, silver everywhere,
But it just may be booby-trapped, so beware!
A million lotteries in there I'd say,
A trillion job cheques and pay.

Nobody knew it,
Nobody at all,
All people thought was under the ground,
Was soil.

Jewels, gold and silver galore
Is under that plain, sandy beach.
As much money as the Queen has and more,
But from here there is a lesson to teach.

There are some treasures, much better than gold,
With money comes greed and hate too,
As people have lived without this,
But your favourite treasure's all up to you.

The most wonderful treasure of all is love,
From your family and God above.
So spread it, there is much more than pounds,
No matter how funny you think it sounds.

Adam Ware (10)
Peter's Hill Primary School

TEACHERS RULE!

It's end of school
It's time to go
We leave the classroom quickly
I hang back
And pretend to pack
My school bag - very slickly

I dare myself to go downstairs
To where the staffroom is
I'm nearly there
But then my dare
Goes wrong in quite a fizz

I hear a teacher calling me
The strictest teacher - Mr Hubbard
The ground's like mash
And in a dash
I hide inside a cupboard

I'm there for quite a long time
But, at last, I try to squeeze out
I fall to the floor
And then run to the door
Hang on! What's this all about?

The doors are locked - it's only four
An hour after school
I'll have to stay
Another day
But until then - *teachers rule!*

James Rowell (10)
Peter's Hill Primary School

HOMEWORK PANIC ATTACK!

Homework, moanwork,
I haven't done my homework.
What will Mrs Abel say?
Will she let me go out to play?

Will she burn me on a steak
Or shoot me with her laser gun?
Will she hang me from a tree,
For everyone around to see?

Or wedge me in a salad burger,
Next to lettuce leaves?
Will she throw me to the lions
Or brand my skin with red-hot irons?

Will she become a purple-crested tantrum,
With sharp yellow teeth and a fearsome face
And horrible green bulging eyes,
Which are a *humungous* size?

Now's the time to hand it in,
I'm sweating buckets beneath my skin.
I watch and wait;
For something terrible to happen . . .

But what's this?
No yellow teeth,
No branding irons or lettuce leaves?
She is just standing there with a stern look on her face
And says, 'Make sure it is done tonight!'

Eleanor Harris (10)
Peter's Hill Primary School

In My Dreams

At night when I go to bed
With the moon sparkling overhead
I dream all kinds of dreams
Especially ones about my brother

I think I'd be an action figure
A little scary but not too much
Every night when he's asleep
I'd aim a missile at his feet
In hope it would cause him pain

Or maybe a toy pirate
Steel all his treasure
In hope for a little pleasure
Of when he wakes up and finds no pocket money in the tin
Would he search in the bin?

Perhaps I'd be an aeroplane model
Hanging from the ceiling
Waiting to drop a bomb
Where would it go?
What would it do?
Would it hit him on the toe?

Oh how I wish this was true
But unfortunately dreams don't come true
I think I'll just stay as me
So I can get my brother my own way
I wonder what would happen

What a dream!
But what if dreams do come true?

Amy Rodgers (10)
Peter's Hill Primary School

The Aqua World

The dull, dark winter, is life on land,
But as for underwater with the sea and the sand.
As you dive in, your life is transformed,
The fish and the creatures, you see what they saw.

While you're exploring the aqua world,
The colours glisten like diamonds and pearls.
I feel like the dolphins are smiling at me,
The whales glide past with nothing but glee.

As the world above is boring and dull,
This life underwater compared is so full.
Starfish, crabs, lobsters too,
If only they could all join the underwater crew.

Caves and shells may be their homes,
The surrounding sounds all different tones.
Salty water swishing about,
It's always peaceful without a doubt.

It's so colourful under the sea,
That's how I see it, happy and free.
I see it as a perfect place,
Filled with creatures that have such grace.

If I could live there permanently,
I'd have to tell what I could see,
With those creatures, I could make friends,
Underwater there's no need for amends.

Anyone young or old,
May ask me how great it is in the aqua world,
And I would answer truthfully,
And ask if they'd like to visit with me.

Cecily Johnson (11)
Peter's Hill Primary School

THE STAFF ROOM

The staff room is a terrible place,
Where teachers go to hide,
It has this nasty, horrible smell
Like the lab of Jekyll and Hyde.

At our break and dinner time,
They go in there to talk,
About those 'bloomin' kids' and 'natterboxes'
Who just won't *shut up!*

As the clock ticks loudly, to go to next lesson,
All coffee, tea gets poured down the drain,
Leaving one poor person
To clean the cups and mugs.

Office members go and take their little break,
Two of them are eating biscuits,
While three sit down and chat,
Leaving one in the corner to read.

At the end of our school day,
Teachers come back to talk.
Some stay in the classroom,
(Most go down the pub!)

The time is now 6 o'clock,
Most of the teachers have gone home,
One or two left in the building,
But not in the staff room, no.

The staff room is now a quiet place,
All peaceful, nice and still,
Until the next day of school,
A tale of the staff room at Peter's Hill!

Richard Clarke (11)
Peter's Hill Primary School

My Dream

I'm standing on the top of a cliff
I can see a beautiful view
Hills, mountains, valleys
The red-hot sun is beaming down
Am I dreaming or awake?

The hills are a dark green
With lots of lively animals
Sheep, lambs, cows, calves
Am I dreaming or awake?

The mountains are blue and purple
With lots of lovely flowers
Daisies, buttercups, daffodils and bluebells
Am I dreaming or awake?

The valleys are bright green
With lots of joyful laughter
Picnics, lovers holding hands and children playing
Am I dreaming or awake?

I'm standing on the edge
Wobbling, worrying, waiting
Then it happens, the edge falls off
Am I dreaming or awake?

I fall down, down, down
Then I go up, up ,up
I've got wings
I fly to the top of the cliff
Am I dreaming or awake?
I'm dreaming!

Louise Pestridge (11)
Peter's Hill Primary School

WONDERING

I'm looking up at the ceiling,
Waiting for a sleepy feeling,
Wondering what I'll dream about,
Maybe meeting people on a roundabout.

I'm looking up at the ceiling,
Waiting for a sleepy feeling,
Wondering what I'll dream about,
That I am famous without a doubt.

I'm looking up at the ceiling,
Waiting for a sleepy feeling,
Wondering what I'll dream about,
When at a Steps concert I will shout.

I'm looking up at the ceiling,
Waiting for a sleepy feeling,
Wondering what I'll dream about,
My grandad getting drunk from his stout.

I'm looking up at the ceiling,
Waiting for a sleepy feeling,
Wondering what I'll dream about,
Having a filling on a dentist's couch.

Finally I'm in a dream,
Many dreams are in my head,
While under my duvet,
Asleep in my bed.

Lauren Hussey (11)
Peter's Hill Primary School

My Mum

My mum is my hero
Rushing around preparing my breakfast, dinner and possibly tea
She gets up, has a good wash and goes into the kitchen
She makes me and my brother lunch and serves our breakfast
Washes the dishes and prepares us for school
My good old mum

When we're at school she works around the house
Hoovering, dusting, cleaning, gardening, washing
At twelve thirty she usually goes to work
Twelve thirty till 5pm
Then arrives and comes and makes her tea
Doing more jobs after tea until bed
That's my hardworking mum.

Matthew Cuff (11)
Peter's Hill Primary School

Rain

Clouds moving over the sky,
They tell us rain is on the way.
Then suddenly raindrops begin to fall
On this chilly autumn day.
Looking through the window
People hurrying by,
With umbrellas held high,
Against the falling misty sky.
When the storm is over,
Gardens refreshed by rain,
Birds sing their song
To greet the sun again.

Zeleka Jade Oakley (10)
Queen Victoria Primary School

SUPER KYE

I saw him in the park,
He was all alone.
But when I turned my back,
Kye was on the phone.

At the speed of lightning,
Kye got up off that chair.
I thought it was powers
Or even a nightmare.

I kept on walking,
I wish I had proof
And when I got back home,
Kye was on my roof.

My feet were on the ground,
Kye was in the sky.
I thought the way he got there,
Was that he would have to fly.

Now I walked up to Kye,
He was right by the bin.
He just walked away
And was the last time I saw him.

Hezekiah Ball (11)
Queen Victoria Primary School

WIND

Ha, ha, he, he,
The wind is playing tricks,
I turn my back to get away,
But around my ears it sticks.

Its teeth are white and gleaming,
His hands are as cold as ice
And when it tries to pull me back,
I shout, 'You're not nice!'

Briony Marshall (11)
Queen Victoria Primary School

My Feet And Me

I'll make this poem short but sweet
I think I'll write about my feet
My feet are big, my toes are small and all in all I'm very tall
That sums me up for one in ten
I think I'll tell you again and again
But I hope that once is enough
If it isn't, well, that's just tough.

Luke Bryan (10)
Queen Victoria Primary School

I Wish I Had A Sister

I'm all alone,
When I play on my own.
I wish I had a sister,
I hate my five brothers,
I ask my mother for advice on what to do.
I wish I had a sister,
I'm always moaning and groaning,
I wish I had a sister.

Billy Hudson (10)
Queen Victoria Primary School

My Hamster

My little hamster's name is Jaws,
He's brown and white with very sharp claws,
He exercises every night in his ball,
Down the length of my very long hall.
He runs around his wheel last thing at night,
Working his legs with all his might.
We go to bed and leave him alone.

If he could speak I'm sure he would moan,
Goodnight Jaws, we'll see you again,
We'll leave you some cheese to eat in your den.

Joseph Slater (10)
Queen Victoria Primary School

Fire

As it starts to leap into the sky,
It grows and grows.
It eats anything in sight,
Not caring if it's a tree or house.
Its flames burn all through the night,
Dancing, twirling and creeping across the landscape.
Flames reaching upwards, sidewards and all around,
Fire, flames burning, red, yellow and orange too,
Finally it leaves nothing but earth and ashes behind.

Rebekah Evans (10)
Queen Victoria Primary School

A Poem About Time!

Time is so little, that we never see!
I now call upon my mind to declare time free
(Let it go) come and see the clock in the hall
It is time for it to strike midnight
The spell is broke
The time is set free for the time-keeper
Now everyone has their own time
Come and look at the time
There is so little time.

Samantha May Brookes (10)
Queen Victoria Primary School

My Hamster

H arriet the hamster
A lways delicate and delightful
M essy, but I don't mind
S oft, furry and feathery
T reasure she could be
E specially likeable to everyone
R unning madly in her ball around the room.

Joshua O'Brien (8)
St Joseph's Catholic Primary School

My Dog, Jemma

(In remembrance of Jemma who died in Jan '01)

Gentle
Always harmless
Playful
Always funny

Calming
Always a friend
Sweetness
Always happy

Loving
Always messy
Helpful
Always joyful

But mostly as golden as can be.

Katie Jeavons (8)
The Ridge Primary School

My Friends

F riends are affectionate, tender and kind
R epenting and helpful, close, likeable
I mpossible to disagree with my friend who likes me
E nduring the years, always there for each other
N eighbourly, good natured, sympathetic companion
D oubting they are not, but kind they are.

Hayley Crump (8)
The Ridge Primary School

My Best Grandad

When Grandad touches me,
Sometimes it feels so very warm,
And when I climb upon his lap,
My memories all return.

His love is lasting forever,
I pray to him for peace.
His voice is just a prayer away,
I talk to him each day.

He's out of pain, I can't feel sad,
That's why my treasure is: my best, big grandad.

Megan Tye (8)
The Ridge Primary School

My Rabbit

T itch is soft, furry and fussy,
I f he was left in the garden all day, every bit of grass would be gone,
T idying up after him is something I don't really like
but I do like fussing him like a pussy,
C ome here, I call at night but he doesn't want to go in his hutch,
H e's cute, furry, soft and fussy, if he was left in the garden all day
all the grass would be eaten away.

Lauren Tibbetts (8)
The Ridge Primary School